Herbs
& Edible Flowers
GARDENING FOR THE KITCHEN

Lois Hole
WITH Earl J. Woods

RECIPES BY

John Butler and
Joyce Pearson, B.H.Ec.

PHOTOGRAPHY BY

Akemi Matsubuchi

ILLUSTRATIONS BY

Donna McKinnon

Herbs and Edible Flowers ❀ *Gardening for the Kitchen*
Lois Hole's *Enjoy Gardening* series #1

PUBLISHED BY HOLE'S
101 Bellerose Drive
St. Albert, Alberta
T8N 8N8

Printed in Canada   5   4   3

Canadian Cataloguing in Publication Data

Hole, Lois, 1933–

  Herbs and edible flowers

  Includes bibliographical references and index.

  ISBN 0-9682791-3-9

  1. Herb gardening. 2. Flower gardening. 3. Plants, Edible. 4. Cookery
(Herbs) 5. Cookery (Flowers) I. Woods, Earl J., 1969– II. Title.
SB351.H5H64 2000   635'.7   C99-911215-5

Photograph on page 55 courtesy of Marney Allen

Film and prepress by Elite Lithographers, Edmonton, Alberta, Canada.

Printed and bound by Quality Color Press, Edmonton, Alberta, Canada.

∞ Printed on acid-free paper.

Contents

Acknowledgements

We wish to send a warm thank-you to all the people who shared their advice and experience in helping us make this book. A special thanks goes out to Pat Yeakley, Russell Food Equipment, Ian Grant, Marney Allen, Melody, Lyra, and Jacob Brown, Jed and Emily Groenenboom, Tracy Lock, Vicki Wilson, the Alberta Crop Diversification Centre South, and the Alberta Crop Diversification Centre North. And of course our deepest thanks go to our wonderful staff here at Hole's for their time, patience, and expertise.

Preface

I'VE ALWAYS ENJOYED GARDENING.
My love for growing things took root
many years ago in my mother's garden, and
continues to this day. My garden has become
such an important part of my life—it's a
constant source of pleasure and inspiration.

Every year, a new crop of young people
discovers—or rediscovers—the joys of making
plants grow. Watching their excitement as they
wander around the greenhouse, choosing their
plants and planning their yards, I remember the
pride we take from a beautiful, well-tended
garden, the pleasure we get from the taste of
homegrown vegetables. These are feelings all
gardeners share!

In my six *Favorites* books, I tried to
make gardening fun and successful by
recommending the best plant varieties.
But while I'm marvelling at the gorgeous
flowers that surround my deck or dishing
out corn picked fresh from the field, I'm
often reminded that enjoying the fruits of
our labours is as delightful as planting and
tending the garden. Hence this new series,
Enjoy Gardening. I hope this series will help
all gardeners, young and old, to get more
enjoyment from your gardens.

I hope you will use *Herbs and Edible Flowers*,
the first book in this series, as a guide to
extending the joys of the garden to your table
and beyond. And I hope that, no matter where
you are or what you're growing, you will
always enjoy gardening.

Introduction

We used to grow dill solely to give away to customers who bought pickling cucumbers.

HAVE YOU NOTICED THE RECENT REVIVAL of interest in herbs? Around the world, herbs are once again in vogue, whether in popular food items like focaccia and soup, household products like shampoo and potpourri, or alternative health practices like aromatherapy and naturopathy. Maybe it's just another aspect of people's passion for plants, gardening, and nature, but it's a trend I welcome. For years, herbs and edible flowers have lived in the realm of gourmets and five-star hotels—it's about time we got back to some of the basics! This book is intended to show you how to enjoy these marvellously versatile plants in your day-to-day meal-planning, festive occasions, and home and garden.

My love of gardening began in my mother's garden in the little town of Buchanan, Saskatchewan. My mother, of solid Swedish stock, didn't use many herbs in her cooking, but I remember that, like every other gardener in Saskatchewan, she had chives growing right outside the back door. She grew some dill for pickling and horseradish for seasoning, but otherwise her energies were focussed on her enormous vegetable garden and her beautiful flower beds.

My mother passed her love for growing things on to me, and I have had the immense good fortune to live out that passion every day of my life. When my husband Ted and I married and moved to a little farm on the banks of the Sturgeon River, near St. Albert, Alberta, we soon discovered that our garden would form the foundation of our business. After a few attempts at traditional farming, Ted and I started selling fresh vegetables from our back porch. Today, our family-run greenhouse is one of the largest garden centres in western Canada. In a single season, we sell more than 5 million bedding plants, perennials, trees, shrubs, and house plants.

In the early days on the farm, the only herbs I grew were mint, chives, thyme, horseradish, parsley,

One gardening task that I really enjoy is watering.

and dill—the same basic herbs that my mother and mother-in-law used. These were definitely not commercial herbs to us; I grew them in the family vegetable garden strictly for seasoning. If customers asked for particular herbs, I directed them to the garden and told them to help themselves. My own use of these herbs was quite traditional—the mint with lamb, the thyme for soups, and the parsley in salads or spaghetti sauce.

We became commercial herb growers almost by accident. In the beginning, we grew dill only to use for pickling. When we sold cucumbers, we gave the dill away to our customers. We thought of it as a weed, and you can't charge money for weeds! Dill took on greater importance when MacDonalds Consolidated Wholesale, Safeway's warehouse operation, called us one day with an emergency. They had a load of cucumbers to ship to the supermarkets, but had no dill to go along with it. Their supply had been infested with aphids. They wanted to pay us $5 per bundle—we couldn't believe it! Happily, we had a bumper crop of healthy dill that year, so Ted grabbed his sickle and headed into the field. He piled the chopped plants into the back of the half-ton truck, and then my sons, Bill and Jim, and I tied the bundles. One of us would grab as much dill as we could wrap our arms around, another would tie the bundle with string, and someone else would pile the bundles on pallets.

Hole's Greenhouses and Gardens, 1999.

3

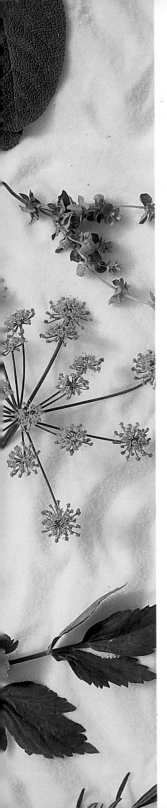

Well, we harvested enough dill to save the day for MacDonalds Consolidated, and they asked us if we would continue supplying them. Of course we couldn't turn down the opportunity, so for some years we grew whole fields full of the delightfully scented annual.

As the years passed, I was exposed to a wide variety of herbs by the new Canadians who came to our farm to buy vegetables. I adapted many of the culinary traditions of these immigrants to my own cooking, which has become all the richer for it. As my own use of herbs increased, so too did our commercial involvement with herbs. Our first attempt to market twelve basic herbs in pots in the greenhouse failed miserably—we were a little ahead of the trend! But today, a full third of our glasshouse is filled with pots of fresh herbs each spring. We carry the basic culinary herbs year-round, but the really unusual varieties show up only briefly in the spring—and our herb devotees know exactly when to find them! We've come a long way from those herbs I once grew in a corner of the garden.

This book is intended to be a handy kitchen and garden reference, based on what I've learned in the garden, input from our staff members, and knowledge shared by many people over the years. What you will find here is practical advice on growing and using 25 of the tastiest, most fragrant, and most beautiful culinary herbs and edible flowers. (I've also discussed 75 other herbs and edible flowers in less detail, later in the book.) You'll discover how, where, and when to plant herbs and edible flowers for the highest yields, and which varieties to grow for the best flavours and scents. We'll also show you how to use them in all kinds of simple and tasty dishes—and we'll give you some tips on presenting them attractively on the table. We'll even suggest other ways to use the bounty of your garden in your kitchen and around your home. And along the way, you'll learn some history and folklore about herbs and edible flowers. We hope that *Herbs and Edible Flowers: Gardening for the Kitchen* will become one of the indispensable volumes in your library—and in your kitchen!

What Is a Herb?

A staple of kitchen gardens for centuries, herbs are often overlooked by gardeners. Many of us think of herbs as low-growing, unobtrusive little plants from which to pick a few leaves now and then to throw in a saucepan or to garnish a dish. But herbs are much more than that.

Herbs are basically defined as non-woody, seed-bearing plants that die back to the ground after flowering—a generally accurate definition, but a little vague because most bedding plants, and many perennials, fall under this category. For the purposes of this book, we define herbs as plants grown primarily for their culinary uses: plants whose leaves, flowers, or seeds can be used as flavouring or garnishes in cooking. Thus, in these pages, you will find annuals, perennials, shrubs, and even vegetables used as culinary herbs.

The distinction between herbs and spices is arbitrary, to say the least. There is no general agreement, and even the dictionary doesn't help much. Although many plants will overlap or defy simple categories, we suggest the following broad definitions:

Herbs usually refer to the soft tissues of plants and tend to be milder in flavour (although there are notable exceptions). Typical examples of herbs include parsley, basil, and thyme.

Spices are usually derived from the tougher parts of plants—the roots, bark, and seeds—and are often strongly flavoured. Typical examples of spices include pepper, cinnamon, nutmeg, and ginger.

Another definition is that herbs are plants of temperate climates, while spices are plants of tropical climates. In this book, we use the catch-all term *herbs* to describe any culinary plants you can use easily in your kitchen.

Edible Flowers

My experience with flowering plants goes back much farther than my experience with herbs, but it's only recently that I've started eating ornamental blossoms. Friends—like Joyce Pearson and John Butler—and professionals—like Chef Allan Fennell at the Hotel Macdonald and the chefs at the Mayfair Golf and Country Club—introduced me to the culinary delights of flowers. The varied tastes of edible flowers and their decorative potential in salads, drinks, and desserts opened up a whole new world of enjoyment for me, making many of my favourite bedding plants and perennials functional as well as beautiful.

The most important point to understand is that not all flowers are edible; in fact, some are very poisonous. When growing flowers for culinary purposes, always choose plants by their Latin botanical names. Common names can vary considerably by language, region, and even over time. When purchasing flower seeds, make sure that the listing in the seed catalogue identifies the variety as edible. It is best to err on the side of caution. If you are not sure a flower is edible, or if you are unsure what part to eat, don't eat it! In most cases, only the petals should be eaten; stems, pistils, and stamens are not usually consumed.

We know relatively little about the nutritional value of edible flowers. We do know, however, that dandelions, marigolds, nasturtiums, roses, and rosehips are all good sources of Vitamin C, and that most edible flowers also contain traces of other important vitamins and minerals. Flowers are about 95% water, making their nutritional content small, but they also tend to be low in calories.

When you first try edible flowers in your recipes, be conservative and use only small quantities until you know that you like the flavour and you're not sensitive to the species. Never use cut-flowers grown for ornamental use in your recipes: they may be treated with pesticides or other chemicals unfit for human consumption. My own rule of thumb is to eat only those flowers I, or others, have grown especially for eating. That way, I can be confident they're safe to eat. Individuals with asthma and allergies should avoid composite flowers like calendula, chrysanthemum, marigolds, and daisies, which may provoke reactions.

100 Herbs and Edible Flowers

The 100 plants included in this book were selected primarily for their culinary uses. We chose plants that we thought gardeners would find most useful in the kitchen and divided our choices into two categories: my 25 favourite herbs and edible flowers, and another 75 suggestions for the more adventurous.

It's important to note the difference between what's edible and what's palatable. Many plants can be eaten, but only some can be enjoyed. For this book, we have chosen herbs and flowers that taste good! Of course, some flavours are acquired tastes, and not everyone will agree about what's tasty and what's not; but we have not recommended any culinary herb or edible flower that isn't widely held to be pleasant-tasting and enjoyable when added to foods or beverages.

Again, we cannot stress enough that not all herbs and flowers are safe to eat. *Never* eat a plant unless you know for certain that it is safe. That means consulting a reliable text or horticultural authority. In this book, we have included only plants that can be consumed safely. We have also included a brief chart of *inedible* plants for your reference (see pages 235-36). And although many herbs and flowers are said to have important medicinal value, we have not recommended any species for such use in this book. We feel that health-related advice is best left to experts. When we mention historical uses of certain herbs and flowers, this information is presented only for the sake of interest and is in no way an endorsement of its use today.

Get your children involved with the garden early: they will cherish the experience for the rest of their lives.

The four-star Hotel Macdonald has its own herb garden.

Herbs, Edible Flowers, and Essential Oils

The reason that herbs and edible flowers smell and taste so wonderful is because they contain essential oils. *Essential* does not mean that the oils are required by the plants; rather, the term refers to their essence, or aroma. These oils are wondrously varied, each a complex chemical compound that imparts specific flavours and scents. They are usually secreted by specialized glands on the leaves, but they can often be found in flowers, too.

Have you ever noticed that many plants give off a stronger scent in hot weather? Essential oils are volatile, meaning that they will vaporize when heated. Sunlight is strong enough to vaporize very small amounts of essential oils, causing plants to emit their characteristic scents. The heat from cooking, however, is much more intense. Strong heat can increase or even destroy the delicate flavours of herbs. Flavours typically increase as the herb tissues break down, releasing the essential oils trapped within the plant's cells. But flavours may be spoiled if oils are lost to excessive heat. For this reason, herbs are often added to dishes in the late stages of cooking. That way, the flavour is at its peak when the food arrives at the table.

Essential oils give plants their delightful scents.

The Recipes

This book contains dozens of recipes written especially for us by Joyce Pearson and John Butler. I am thrilled that they have agreed to share their expertise to help you enjoy herbs and edible flowers in new and exciting ways. Joyce Pearson has been a friend for many years and has introduced me to many new tastes. Many of you will know her from her former role as the Home Service Director at the Blue Flame Kitchen, where she reached thousands of homes with her wonderful recipes. John Butler, a certified master chef, teaches culinary arts at Edmonton's Northern Alberta Institute of Technology.

There he is passing on his knowledge to chefs in training, through a blend of theory, technique, and practice. I asked John and Joyce to come up with quick, easy, enjoyable ways to use herbs and edible flowers in the kitchen and in the home, and we were all amazed by the results.

Our purpose in including recipes in this book was to help you get more enjoyment from herb gardening. Many of us grow herbs each year without using them to their fullest. The recipes in this book

range from the simple and everyday to the formal and exotic. Many dishes draw upon diverse cultural influences and reflect the adventurous spirit of cooking today. Others are more traditional, exploring the rich potential of herbs in familiar settings. I encourage you to use the herbs and edible flowers in your garden whenever you can.

Please take the time to read the section In the Kitchen (pages 27 to 32), in which John and Joyce provide great advice on introducing herbs and edible flowers to your cooking. And remember, you can make these recipes year-round, even when your garden is not flourishing. Many grocery stores now stock a wide range of fresh herbs in the produce section, and dried or frozen herbs can be used in place of fresh if necessary.

Take advantage of a bright windowsill and grow herbs indoors year-round. Over the years, Ted grew many plants on this old heat register.

The Herb Garden

One of the great joys of herbs is that you don't need a huge garden to grow them. Most herbs will thrive in patio pots and other containers, and many will do well indoors in a sunroom or on a bright windowsill.

For convenience plant your herb garden close to the kitchen.

The Indoor Herb Garden

Growing herbs indoors can present a challenge, but if flowering houseplants flourish in your home, most herbs should grow well there too. Your indoor herb garden can be as small or large as your available space and light will allow. Many people grow a small trough of common herbs (e.g., basil, oregano, and parsley) on the kitchen windowsill; others pamper a tender shrub or dwarf tree (e.g., rosemary or bay laurel) in a sunny living-room or dining-room window. Indoor herbs won't usually grow as large their outdoor counterparts, and they may not set flowers, but their flavours will be bright and even, and their leaves and stems will be more tender.

The biggest challenge for indoor herbs is getting enough light. Herbs need at least 5 hours of direct sunlight per day, which means placing them in a south- or west-facing window, as close as possible to the glass. Don't forget to turn the pots from time to time so that all sides of the plant receive light. Make sure your windows are clean: dirty windows can significantly reduce light reaching your plants.

Water indoor herbs regularly, but don't bother misting them. Many herbs are susceptible to powdery mildew, which can be aggravated by misting. Fertilize every 2 to 3 weeks with dilute 20-20-20 (¼ strength). Harvest regularly to keep the plant tidy and productive, and you will enjoy the flavours of summer on even the coldest winter days.

The Outdoor Herb Garden

Almost any herb can be grown successfully in your garden, whether you seed directly, propagate from an established plant, or purchase young plants from a garden centre. Herbs need the same basic care as any other garden plants, although some are fussier than others. But remember, herbs are relatively inexpensive—you can afford to experiment a little, take a few risks. Set out the hardy ones early, baby the tender ones for a few weeks, then get growing!

Planting a culinary herb garden is a little different than planting an ornamental garden. Aesthetics are important, but I believe that convenience, room for easy maintenance, and optimum growing conditions are the primary objectives. If your culinary garden is close to your kitchen, so much the better. Herbs and edible flowers are often harvested in the midst of dinner preparations. I grow most of my herbs close to the house for the sake of convenience. For example, a pot of pansies sits outside my back door and adds both cheerful colour and a quick garnish for salads and desserts. For easy access, herb beds should be no more than 1 m across. Harvest and maintenance become difficult with wider beds, unless you set in stepping stones in strategic locations.

Intersperse herbs with edible flowers to create an attractive and functional display. Parsley makes a wonderful border, and a mass planting of roses is both lovely and functional. But be sure not to mix very invasive plants with less-competitive plants, and don't let tall-growing herbs shade out their smaller neighbours.

Roses and sorrel look great planted together.

Most herbs grow well in containers.

Grower's Edge

Vermiculite is mined rock, heated until it resembles an accordian when viewed under a microscope. This structure allows vermiculite to hold moisture and nutrients very well, and it is also a good source of potassium. **Blonde peat** is simply peat moss that hasn't undergone much decomposition. It holds moisture extremely well, while also allowing air to get to the roots. **Wetting agents** are substances that allow the growing medium to absorb water more easily. **Pores** are the spaces not occupied by the soilless mix—spaces that air, water, and the roots will fill. A growing medium with high porosity supports plants better than one with low porosity.

Growing Herbs in Containers

Most herbs and edible flowers thrive in containers and patio pots—in fact, for many plants, I encourage you to grow them this way. Finicky plants like basil, tender perennials like rosemary, and aggressive plants like mint are excellent candidates for container growing. Most edible flowers can also be grown in hanging baskets, moss planters, and patio pots. Try planting in combinations for spectacular contrasts of colour and growth habit. How about a clump of chives surrounded by a colourful ring of pansies, or a potted sunflower with a base of nasturtiums? Let your imagination be your guide!

Years ago my husband Ted convinced me to use soilless mix in containers instead of garden soil, and I'm glad he made the effort. Soilless mix is by far the best growing medium for herbs in pots. It's lightweight and sterile, it doesn't get compacted, it's free of weeds, disease, and insects, and it's reusable. It also holds moisture, but drains well. Soilless mixes come in a variety of blends. Ingredients may include sphagnum peat moss, composted bark, coconut fibre, perlite, vermiculite, and old newspaper pulp. Many mixes even have slow-release fertilizer incorporated into them.

One of the big advantages to growing in containers is that weeding is a snap. If you've used soilless mix in the containers, you may never encounter a weed at all. If a weed does emerge, you can easily pull it out by hand before it gets big enough to compete with your plants.

Planning Your Herb Garden

Herb gardens are unique in that they combine the form of traditional flowerbeds and the functionality of a vegetable garden. Some gardeners like to plan their gardens in meticulous detail. I don't plant that way—I've always preferred function over form—but for those of you who have a hankering to recreate a classical herb garden or design the perfect formal herbscape, here are a few pointers from our landscape designer, Chris Hamilton.

Whenever I start a new project, I begin with a simple drawing of the yard. I note the shady areas, fences, trees, pathways, house and garage, other permanent fixtures, and orientation of the yard. I also note variations in soil type.

Then the yard owners and I discuss an overall style. Formal or informal? Modern or classic? Mixed beds or mass plantings? We talk about how long the project will take to complete and what level of commitment maintenance will require. Are they avid gardeners or would they prefer something easy to keep up? What are their longer-term plans for the area? Are they looking for perennial solutions or do they want to renew the beds annually? Together we come to a plan that suits the yard, the owners' available time, and the budget.

Experiment with your herb garden. Use borders and varying levels to add visual interest.

Here's a basic plan for a kitchen herb garden, prepared by my colleague Maggie Clayton. Note the stepping stones, which encourage visitors to experience the visual and aromatic garden as well as its edible offerings. This plan permits multiple plantings of fast-growing varieties, with big plants like dill and coriander in the back so the garden still looks lovely even after the harvest. Containers allow tender perennials like bay and cardamom to come in for the winter, and confine aggressive species like mint. This garden could be accented with strongly scented herbs, like mother of thyme between the stepping stones, to add alluring fragrances and with various edible flower varieties to lend additional colour and interest. Many people grow herbs solely for their scent—a herb doesn't have to be harvested to be enjoyed.

KITCHEN HERBS:

A. DILL
B. SAGE
C. CORIANDER
D. BASIL
E. CHIVES
F. PARSLEY
G. OREGANO
H. THYME
IN POTS:
J. BAY
K. MINT
L CARDAMOM

The possibilities are endless. The important point is that planning your garden isn't complicated if you take it step by step and use your imagination.

12 -D
DECK
J
K
K
L
2-A B 2-C
E F F G
H
STEPS
PATIO

Planting Herbs and Edible Flowers

How Much to Plant

In the accounts that follow, we suggest how many plants of each variety you should grow, based on what we predict an average household will use. As it is impossible to predict tastes, these are meant as rough guides. For most varieties, we recommend you grow at least two. But if you really like a certain herb, plant more than we recommend: use your own knowledge to guide your choices. Season by season, you'll learn how productive each variety is and how much you tend to harvest, so you can adjust your planting accordingly.

Remember that herbs and edible flowers make great ornamentals as well as delicious culinary plants. They're inexpensive, easy to replace, and fairly low-maintenance. Don't worry about planting too many—you'll enjoy their presence in your garden even if you don't harvest as much as you expect.

If you're seeding herbs and flowers directly into your garden, don't be afraid to sow thicker than recommended on the package. The weather may take an unexpected turn and claim part of your crop, and birds, bugs, and other garden raiders will inevitably take their portion. You can always share with friends and family what you don't use yourself, and most herbs can be easily stored for later consumption.

When to Plant

I'm impatient with our short—and sometimes unpredictable—season. I generally find it is a better use of my energy to work with young plants from the greenhouse. However, many herbs can be grown successfully from seed or started in the house and then planted into the garden once the weather starts to stay warm.

Some herbs are hardier than others and can take a little frost. With that in mind, take advantage of the hardy herbs and plant early! But protect delicate

Grower's Edge

In general, herb seeds have a short storage life—and the longer they're kept in storage, the lower the germination rates are likely to be. If you must store seeds for extended periods, keep them in a sealed jar in a cool, dry, dark place. Warm, humid conditions cause seeds to deteriorate rapidly. I store seeds in resealable plastic containers with dessicant packs to absorb moisture.

herbs by waiting until soil and air temperatures are warm and the risk of frost is low.

Before young plants are planted in the garden, they must be acclimatized to the outdoors. Plants grown indoors have soft stems and leaves that need to be toughened up. We call this hardening off. Once daytime temperatures are regularly above freezing, set young plants outside in a spot that gets only indirect sunlight and is sheltered from the wind; bring the plants back indoors each night over a period of five to seven days. On the seventh day, plant them into the garden or container.

Herbs must be harvested at their peak to capture their best flavour. Plants that over-mature can get woody and tough. Since many herbs will reach their prime well before the growing season ends, it pays to plant these herbs at least twice over the course of a season. My daughter-in-law Valerie sows fast-growing herbs (those that mature in less than 70 days) 2 to 3 times per season at 2 to 3-week intervals.

Starting Seed Indoors

Not all herbs and edible flowers can be grown successfully from seed, but many can. If you enjoy growing seedlings, try starting seeds at home. It's the most inexpensive way to grow herbs and flowers, and it often allows you a wider range of choices.

To start seedlings, fill a seedling flat (available at any garden centre) to within 1 cm of the top with good-quality seedling mix. Don't use garden soil: it tends to harden quickly and often contains diseases or other pests. Plant seeds shallowly—to about the depth of the seed's thickness. Plant 3 seeds in each cell in the flat for larger seeds, 8 to 10 seeds per cell for fine seeds. Cover the seeds with a thin layer of vermiculite, then water with a misting bottle just to moisten the soil. You don't want to dislodge the seeds.

Cover the flat with a plastic dome (often sold with flats) to create a humid environment, then place it in a warm location (such as on top of the refrigerator, near a radiator, or on a heated table). Use grow lights to encourage germination and growth. Tag each flat with variety and date planted.

No matter where you live, the phrase "date of the average last spring frost" means the same thing. It's the date when there is a 50% chance of frost. The date of the average last spring frost in my area is May 6th; that means there's a better than 50% chance of a frost before May 6th, a 50% chance of a frost on May 6th, and a less than 50% chance after May 6th. The risk of frost continues to diminish as the season progresses towards summer and increases once again as summer turns to fall.

Never handle seedlings by the stems when transplanting—stems are easily crushed. Always handle by the cotyledons (seed leaves) or, if the seedlings are in clumps, by the root ball.

Check your flats twice daily, morning and night. Do not allow the seedling mix to dry out, but don't overwater. As soon as the seedlings begin to emerge, move the flat to a cooler (but not cold!) location. When the second set of leaves emerges, begin applying diluted plant-starter fertilizer (e.g., 10–52–10 at ¼ strength).

Some herbs germinate quickly; others require great patience. See the chart on page 237 for seeding and transplanting dates.

Propagation by Cutting

Some herbs must be vegetatively propagated—that is, grown from cuttings from established plants. Vegetatively propagated plants are like clones, each one genetically identical to its mother plant. (Plants propagated by seed are genetically variable, like children.) Growing from cuttings is a little more complicated than growing from seed, but I encourage you to give it a try.

Stocky, vigorous, pest-free plants produce top-quality cuttings. New, non-flowering growth is best: it is less likely to harbour disease than older growth, and it sets roots readily. The best cuttings generally come from the midpoint of the shoot. Clip just below a set of leaves.

Take cuttings from the mother plant and allow them to dry for at least an hour. Drying allows the wound to form a protective layer over the cut end. Dip the stems in rooting hormone before placing the cuttings in soilless mix. Leave the top two sets of leaves in place but clip off any leaves near soil level. Mist the cuttings to reduce moisture loss and put them in a warm spot. Rooting takes 1 to 2 weeks, and it takes about 6 weeks to develop a fully branched plant from a cutting, although some herbs will take longer and a few will root more quickly.

Using a dial seeder is a handy, inexpensive way to ensure the even spacing of seeds.

Where to Plant

Sunlight

Most herbs do best in full sun, meaning that they need at least 5 hours of direct sunlight per day. A garden located on the south or west side of your house is ideal. Plant against a wall or fence to provide some shelter from strong winds and to boost day and night temperatures by a couple of degrees. (But leave room between the plants and the wall for air to circulate.)

If you're growing herbs in containers, the same rules apply. If you have the patience, you can even move herbs in pots around the garden to follow the sun.

Soil

Most herbs grow best in moderately fertile, well-drained soil—a nice, friable loam. Soil should be nearly neutral or just slightly acidic; a pH between 6 and 7 is about right. Note that excessively fertile soils can reduce herbs' production of essential oils. Too much nitrogen in particular can produce weak-flavoured leaves and stems. Avoid low or wet areas.

If you have excessively poor soil, there are ways to amend it. Add sand, perlite, peat moss, compost, well-rotted manure, or even fresh potting soil to enrich the existing soil. Prepare soil in the spring, working the amendments about 15 cm into the earth. Turn the soil over with a shovel, break up lumps, and remove large rocks. Soil can also be turned over again in the fall, leaving large clumps of earth at the surface. This exposes more of the soil to freezing and thawing, improving the soil structure. Use a rototiller if you prefer, taking care not to till too finely: fine soil tends to get compacted, and it is also more likely than coarse soil to be washed away by rain. A smooth, lump-free seedbed is a sure way to encourage rapid and even germination of seeds.

Grower's Edge

Full sun in December is entirely different than full sun in June. In my area of the country, days in mid-June are 17 hours long—but in December, we get only 8 hours of sunlight per day. June sun is also 4 times more intense than December sun. Taking day length and light intensity into account, the light energy that reaches herbs in June can be 10 times than that in December.

Herbs grow best in a warm, sheltered, sunny location.

If you are not planting into the garden, be sure to use a soilless mix in your containers (see page 12).

Spacing

The eventual yield of your harvest depends, in part, upon the number of plants you grow in a given area. It is better to provide extra space between plants if at all possible. Well-spaced plants tend to be more vigorous: there's less competition for soil nutrients, less shading from other plants, and fewer problems with disease.

When you plant in containers, be sure not to crowd too many plants into a single pot. Many species do best grown in a container by themselves. If you plant herbs and edible flowers together in containers, choose species whose height and spread complement one another—you don't want big, tall borage plants shading out your dainty creeping thyme.

Care and Nurture

Watering

Watering is absolutely the most important job in the garden, a task that requires dedication and a keen eye. Most herbs are more drought tolerant than vegetables, basil being a notable exception. But herbs should not be allowed to dry out, especially during their early stages of growth. Keep the soil moist but not wet.

The first thing I do after breakfast is grab my hose and head out into the garden. I water early in the morning so that the plants have a chance to dry during the day. If you water in the afternoon, you lose much of the water to evaporation, and watering at night makes plants vulnerable to disease. Remember to water the base of the plant, not the leaves, to avoid spreading disease, and be careful not to splash soil on plants.

Most herbs and edible flowers are quite thirsty, so give them a good soaking every other day. When the weather is hot and dry, I water every day. Don't depend on rainfall. Containers may need to be

Grower's Edge

When using a hose to water, attach a good water wand, one with a shut-off valve so that you won't have to run back to the tap to turn off the water. Water wands equipped with a flood nozzle provide a nice, even spray that won't bowl plants over but delivers lots of water to the roots.

watered once a day or more! When watering pots or hanging baskets, stop when water begins to drain out the bottom.

Fertilizer

Fertilizing herbs and edible flowers is pretty simple. Give them 10-52-10 once a week for the first 3 weeks, then use 20-20-20 once a week for the rest of the season.

Don't fertilize perennials after August 15. The nitrogen in fertilizer encourages new soft-tissue growth. New growth late in the season can make plants susceptible to freezing.

Fertilize most herbs once a week after they're established.

Pinching, Deadheading, and Pruning

Pinching

Many herbs need to be pinched regularly to keep their energy focussed on leaf production rather than flowering or stem growth. Pinch off the growing tip to force the plant to take a rounder, bushier shape. The plant will be sturdier and more productive as a result.

Deadheading

Deadhead your edible flowers regularly to promote continuous blossoming. Deadheading—picking off dead and dying flowers—diverts energy to new, young flowers and away from seed production. I deadhead every day—the plants look so much better for it, and I'm rewarded with many more blooms.

Pruning

Some herbs, especially shrubby species, will require pruning to maintain their shape and divert energy to new growth. Prune regularly to remove damaged, diseased, and dead stems. Use small clippers or even scissors to prune herbs.

Grower's Edge

Be sure to use a fertilizer that contains chelated iron. *Chelate* is the Greek word for "claw." The iron is held in a claw-like chemical structure, making it more readily available to plants. Herbs generally have a high iron requirement, and pale, veiny upper growth is a sure sign of iron deficiency.

Pinching promotes bushy growth.

19

To kill germinating weeds, gently stir the soil surface with an upturned rake about a week after seeding.

Grower's Edge

Even under favourable growing conditions, some weed seeds will not germinate. Such seeds are termed dormant. Weeds like wild oats and lamb's quarters produce a high proportion of dormant seeds. Dormancy helps plants avoid devastation when severe frosts or droughts hit; although many plants may die, there will still be seeds safe within the earth for germination next year. Seeds can remain dormant for many years, some requiring multiple environmental triggers—periods of freezing and thawing or certain temperatures— before they will germinate.

Weeds

Weeds compete with herbs and edible flowers for space, water, nutrients, and light; they can substantially reduce your harvest. The best time to control weeds is early in the spring, before they become established.

Perennial weeds like thistle and quack grass must be controlled prior to planting in the garden. These weeds have long, tough rhizomes that must be completely destroyed or they will form new plants. Rototill or turn the soil over often. Work the soil on hot, windy days: the wind will help to dry the weeds out. Don't plant your garden until the perennial weeds have been banished, or you'll face a continuing battle.

One of the most effective methods of weed control prior to planting is spraying with RoundUp (glyphosate). Don't work the soil, but water the ground often to encourage the weeds to come up. Ten days prior to planting or seeding your crops, when the weeds are a few centimetres tall, spray with RoundUp. This treatment will significantly reduce your weed problems while still retaining good soil moisture and organic matter. RoundUp is a safe herbicide when used properly: it breaks down quickly and will not contaminate edible plants.

Destroy annual weeds as they emerge by pulling them out by hand or slicing them off with a hoe. Pull a stirrup hoe through the earth to sever the root. Weed on dry days. Many weed seedlings can re-root if they are pulled when the soil is moist.

Never let annual weeds set seed. Weeds that have gone to seed should never be placed in the compost heap—if you do this, you'll spread their seeds when you spread your compost.

A quick way to control weeds is with black landscape fabric. This porous, woven plastic material allows water to penetrate to the soil beneath it, but prevents weeds from growing. Cover your garden with fabric, slicing an X through it for each plant to poke through. Cut extra-large holes for the perennials that you want to spread. Use an eye-pleasing mulch to hide the fabric. Crushed rock, bark, or moss all work well.

Pests and Disease

Pests and diseases present some of the greatest challenges to gardeners. I follow four rules to help me decide what to do with troubled plants. First, try removing the problem. Remove any visible bugs or diseased plant parts. If the problem isn't severe, simply picking off the bugs or cutting off the diseased leaves may do the trick.

If that doesn't work and it's early in the season, start again. I have solved many pest problems by simply tossing out the plant and starting over. Reseeding or buying a new plant is less work and can actually save money in the long run, since you're not spending money on pest control.

Your next option is to spray, if the plant is valuable or the problem is still at a stage where an effective control is available. If you spray, use only pesticides recommended for edible plants. And remember that an "organic" label does not guarantee that the product is safer or works any better than a "chemical" pesticide. When spraying, make sure the product makes contact with all parts of the plant.

Landscape fabric will help control weeds, retain moisture, and keep plants clean.

When all else fails, make plans for next year. Perhaps the soil conditions can be changed for the next growing season. Try relocating the plants: changing locations from year to year can throw off pests that overwinter in the soil close to their potential hosts. (Be sure to move plants of a different family into a pest-prone location—a bug that attacks dill will probably attack fennel but may avoid pansies.) Make sure the spot isn't too shady or too sunny for the plant: weak, soft growth or burned leaves render a plant vulnerable to pests. You can try planting insect-repelling plants like marigolds and garlic nearby. You can also choose varieties bred for superior pest and disease resistance.

When I see a disease like powdery mildew, my first response is to remove the affected leaves.

Review your cultivation methods. Are your plants getting enough water and fertilizer? The best way to prevent pests and disease is to raise healthy plants—they are much more resistant than weak, stressed plants. Finally, clean up your garden in the fall. Remove any diseased plants and debris, to minimize the chance of problems next year. Never throw diseased plants into your compost pile: the disease organisms may spread and infect other plants that come in contact with the compost. However, you can usually compost plants with insect infestations, since the heat of composting tends to kill off the pests.

Division

The best time to divide perennial herbs is early in the spring, while the weather is still cool. Gently dig out the plants when they send up their first shoots. Cut the crown vertically and divide the plant into sections, each with a nice clump of roots. Wash or brush the dirt off the roots, and plant.

Bringing Plants Indoors for the Winter

When the weather starts to turn cool, it's time to bring tender perennials into the house for the winter. Bay laurel, cardamom, pineapple sage, lemon verbena, and rosemary are good candidates for bringing indoors. The plants enjoy the pampering they receive indoors, and you get healthier, more advanced growth. If they are looking good, you can also bring in smaller herbs such as basil, chives, marjoram, and winter savory. But remember, these plants are easily started from seed or young plants, and are often not worth saving from year to year. New plants will also help you avoid pest problems.

Spray for insects, then isolate from other houseplants for a few days. Harvest from these plants more sparingly through the winter. The plants will need to be hardened off again in spring as they return to the garden.

Aphids are prolific pests but fairly easy to control if caught early.

Harvesting

Most herbs can be harvested throughout the growing season. Use a sharp knife or sharp scissors to harvest: dull blades can damage plants and inhibit regrowth. Cut in such a way as to keep the herb looking healthy and avoid any woody growth. Don't leave bare stems sticking out. Harvest what you need as you need it, but never take more than a third of the foliage at once unless you plan to harvest the entire plant. Remember, some leaves must be left in place in order for the plant to continue growing.

The best time to harvest the foliage of most herbs is just prior to blooming. Foliage should be clipped in the morning, after the dew has evaporated but before the day becomes too hot. If you let them form, the flowers of culinary herbs are also safe to eat. The basic rule is that if the leaf is edible, so is the flower.

Pick edible flowers immediately before you need them: they don't store well. The flavours of flowers peak in the early morning and late afternoon, when volatile oils are at their highest levels. After picking, gently rinse flowers to remove dust and dirt, then drain them on dry towels.

Harvest herbs in the mid-morning before the day gets too hot.

When seedheads change colour (usually to reddish brown) and turn dry, it's time to harvest seeds. Cut them on a hot, dry day: moist seeds are prone to rapid deterioration in storage.

To harvest the roots of annuals, simply dig them up at the end of the growing season. To harvest the roots of perennials, dig up no more than a third of the root mass just as the leaves start to form in the spring or as they start to die in the fall. You must leave some stored nutrients for the plant if you want it to keep producing. Gently rinse the soil off roots before drying, but don't use a brush: the bristles can damage the tissue.

For Best Flavour

In the accounts that follow, you will see a section called For Best Flavour, in which we give tips for capturing herbs and edible flowers at their peak. In some cases, you get the best flavour at a specific

Grower's Edge

Put washed herbs in your salad spinner and give them a quick, gentle whirl to remove excess water before cooking, freezing, or drying.

point in a plant's life-cycle. Don't let that prevent you from harvesting throughout the growing season! The herbs and edible flowers in this book taste great all season long; but if you want to capture the richest aromas for a specific reason (e.g., freezing or drying), this information can help you plan your harvesting cycle.

Preserving the Harvest

Whenever possible, use fresh herbs or flowers: they taste better and have a more even consistency. Most herbs can be preserved easily by drying or freezing, but edible flowers are fragile and won't last long without immediate treatment.

Refrigerating flowers

Edible flowers keep poorly, even if refrigerated. Don't cut them until the very last minute! If you must cut blossoms in advance, treat them like cut-flowers: put the long, freshly cut stems in ice water and refrigerate. Use the flowers as quickly as possible—they will last only a few hours.

See pages 134–135 for methods for crystallizing flowers, an easy way to preserve most edible blossoms.

Flower Preparation

Here's how to prepare edible flowers for use in cooking, baking, and decoration. Snip flowers as required. Soak in slightly salted water for 15 minutes to ensure cleanliness and freedom from insects. Drain thoroughly on towels. For recipes that require flower petals, snip off the bases and scatter petals onto fresh towels. Dry only to remove surface moisture on the petals then refrigerate until required. For recipes that require whole flowers, place cleaned flowers on a towel-covered plate, cover tightly with plastic wrap, and refrigerate until needed. Remember to use only flowers that you know have been grown for culinary use.

Freeze herbs in resealable plastic bags.

Drying herbs

Drying is an easy way to preserve most herbs (although some herbs, and most edible flowers, do not dry well). To air-dry herbs, remove all soil and roots, wash and gently dry the foliage, and hang in bunches upside down in a dark, well-ventilated area, such as a spare room with the curtains shut and the door open. Another method is to spread the foliage in a thin layer on screens or framed cheesecloth and

Drying herbs make an attractive display.

cover with a single thickness of paper towel.

You can also use your home appliances to dry herbs. To dry herbs in the oven, spread them in a thin layer on a cookie sheet and bake at no more than 48°C until the leaves are dry and crispy. To dry herbs in a micro-wave oven, spread clean sprigs in an even layer between sheets of paper towel and heat on high setting for 2 minutes. Rearrange the herbs, cover with fresh paper towel, and heat for 2 more minutes, checking every 30 seconds and removing herbs as they dry. (The time will vary with the amount and type of herbs.) Leave on the counter to cool and dry completely, then store in clean, labelled glass jars in a cool, dark area. To use a fruit and vegetable dehydrator, follow the manufacturer's instructions and check the herbs frequently. Over-drying will reduce their colour and aroma.

Store dried herbs in plastic bags or glass jars in a cool, dry, dark location.

A sprig of fresh mint enhances lemonade.

Freezing

Most herbs can be preserved well by freezing. We recommend two methods, one for whole leaves and one for chopped leaves and stems.

Method 1✳ Rinse herbs in cold water and shake dry. Remove large, tough stems; leave small, tender stems attached. Dip the leaves quickly in olive oil to seal in their flavour and put them in plastic bags, being careful not to crowd them. Store bags in an isolated part of the freezer or in a sealed container. If they are crushed or brushed too often (through ordinary freezer use), their essential oils will be lost.

Method 2✳ Wash and finely chop fresh herbs. Pack into plastic ice-cube trays, fill with water, and freeze until solid. Remove cubes from trays and store in labelled freezer bags for up to 6 months. Drop cubes into cooking pots as desired (e.g., for soups, stews, and casseroles).

A lovely way to preserve edible flowers is to make flower ice-cubes. Simply freeze a single blossom in each cube. You can also preserve small sprigs of herbs in this manner to add a decorative touch to summer drinks and festive punches—imagine lemonade with mint or coolers with borage flowers!

Other methods

There are many other ways to capture the flavours of herbs and edible flowers, such as flavoured butters, oils, and vinegars. Please see pages 28 to 32 for more suggestions.

Use a food dehydrator to dry herbs.

In the Kitchen with John and Joyce

The Kitchen Garden

Herbs, like spices, have a place in every kind of cooking. Appetizers, soups, salads, vegetables, stews, main courses, biscuits, cakes, desserts, and beverages can all benefit from the thoughtful addition of herbs and edible flowers. Herbs are used to flavour foods in all the world's great cuisines and, on their own or in combination, form the essential flavours of simple and elegant dishes alike. Cooking with herbs and edible flowers turns food into a sensuous experience.

Herbs vary in their flavour intensity, some—such as rosemary, sage, thyme, savory, and tarragon—being much more pungent than others. Pungent herbs should be used sparingly, while mildly flavoured herbs—such as parsley, basil, chervil, and chives—can be used more liberally.

A good kitchen-herb garden should contain the basics: chervil, chives, cilantro, dill, marjoram, mint (several varieties), oregano, parsley, rosemary, sage, tarragon, and thyme. Once you have these species established, try different varieties of each one and introduce new herbs as you discover them.

All herbs are best used fresh! However, drying or freezing your own herbs will certainly enhance your cooking over the long winter months. Dried and frozen herbs, and other herbal preserves like oils, vinegars, and butters, can be kept for months. A little effort at preserving your favourite herbs is a good investment of time and resources.

Have fun with your herb garden! Don't be afraid to try a new flavour or to add a new herb or flower to an old, familiar recipe. Experiment with your garden to discover your own favourite flavour combinations. Just remember that combining too many pungent herbs in one dish may lead to more conflict than harmony.

Did you know that the worst place in the kitchen to store herbs is also the place we generally keep them? That's right, the spice rack above your stove is a poor storage place for herbs. The heat and moisture from cooking rob herbs of their essential oils, making them deteriorate quickly. Store your herbs away from the heat, in the pantry or a cupboard; take them out as necessary and return them when you're done.

A purée of sorrel is an excellent accompaniment to omelettes.

Getting the Best from Herbs

Foods that enhance the flavours of fresh herbs and edible flowers include fresh-ground pepper; high-quality extra-virgin olive oil, walnut oil, and grape-seed oil; fresh squeezed lemon and lime juice; butter; top-quality Dijon and whole-grain mustards; and fresh, top-quality meats, poultry, and fish.

Some Basic Herb Recipes

The best way to start using herbs and edible flowers regularly is by learning some simple preparations. These basics will form the foundation for your daily use of herbs and edible flowers. The methods are simple and the products are delicious! We hope you'll make these recipes often.

Before you make these or any other recipes, read through the complete method and assemble the ingredients. Clean your workspace and do any advance preparation *before* you begin cooking.

Basic herb vinegar

Infused vinegar adds an unexpected flavour to food. Use alone or with a small amount of good-quality oil to dress a green salad, vegetable salad, warm potato salad, or dish of freshly sliced cucumbers. Add a dash to steamed vegetables, sandwich fillings, or fruit salad. A spoonful does wonders in soups, stews, and bean dishes. Gravies, sauces, and casseroles will all take on a unique and zesty flavour. Best of all, it's better for you than salt!

1 cup	250 mL	herb or herb/flower/ vegetable combination
2 cups	500 mL	vinegar

Master method ✳ The herbs must be very well washed and dried before starting. Bruise the herbs by crushing lightly with a spoon or mortar and pestle to release maximum flavour. Put herbs in a freshly sterilized glass jar. Cover with vinegar and steep in a warm area for up to 3 weeks. Shake gently every few days. When flavour has fully developed, strain through coffee filters. Heat to a gentle simmer, *but do not boil.* Bottle in freshly sterilized bottles with tight lids. Store in a cool, dark area. The flavour will remain excellent for 3 to 12 months, depending on the combination of herbs. This recipe may be doubled or tripled.

Herb vinegar variations to try

Single-herb vinegars, such as tarragon or thyme, are delightful, but herbs in combination can create spectacular culinary effects. Be careful to choose flavours that complement one another and not to use too many herbs at once. Too many competing flavours can confuse the palate.

* **Italian Vinegar:** Fill jar with a combination of oregano, basil, thyme, marjoram, a small amount of rosemary, peeled garlic cloves, and black peppercorns. Use red wine vinegar for best results, although white vinegar also yields a good product. Follow *master method*, above.

* **Pot of Flowers Vinegar:** Fill jar with 3 yellow chrysanthemums, 3 yellow or orange marigolds, 10 to 12 nasturtium leaves with flowers, 1 thin piece lemon, and ½ tsp. (2.5 mL) white peppercorns. Add white wine vinegar for best flavour. Follow *master method*, above.

* **Country French Savoury Vinegar:** Fill jar with a combination of tarragon, marjoram, thyme or savory, oregano, rosemary, sage, and peeled garlic cloves. Add red wine or apple cider vinegar for best flavour. Follow *master method*, above. Hint: German thyme is very mild, while Wedgewood thyme is intense and spicy.

* **English Mint Vinegar:** Fill jar with a combination of English or garden mint, a few very thin lemon slices, chervil or marjoram, chives, 1 bay leaf, and 3 or 4 whole allspice or black peppercorns. Add white wine or Japanese rice wine vinegar for best flavour. Follow *master method*, above. Hint: Experiment with mint varieties. Ginger mint, lime mint, spearmint, and grapefruit mint all yield great flavour.

Lemon verbena is a great addition to a cup of tea.

Choosing a base vinegar

When you make flavoured vinegars, choose your base vinegar carefully. Each type has its own distinctive qualities; use a vinegar that will support and enhance, not compete with, the flavours you're preserving.

* *White wine vinegar has a soft, delicate flavour and is excellent with fruits and delicately flavoured herbs.*

* *Red wine vinegar has a much fuller, richer flavour and is a good choice for more aromatic herbs, such as thyme, savory, and rosemary.*

* *Apple cider vinegar has a light flavour and works well for herb/vegetable combinations.*

* *Chinese or Japanese rice wine vinegar has a delicate flavour and should be used with light herbs and flowers.*

* *White, or spirit, vinegar will yield a harsher flavour but is inexpensive and suitable for robust flavours, such as garlic, hot peppers, rosemary, and strongly flavoured edible flowers.*

Herb butter

Herb butter is an easy way to add instant flavour to almost any dish. Use herb butters on savoury breads and biscuits, for sandwich spreads, for sautéing meat and fish, melted over vegetables, blended into sauces, and as an accompaniment for grilled seafood and meats—almost anywhere you might use plain butter. You can tailor single-flavour butters to complement your table or experiment to find your own favourite blends—there are hundreds of combinations!

If you enjoy herb butters, be sure to try flower-petal butters, too. See page 154 for recipes.

1 lb.	454 g	butter (unsalted butter OK)
2 to 3 tbsp.	30 to 45 mL	finely chopped fresh herbs
lemon juice and pepper, to taste (optional)		

Soften the butter in a large bowl. Add the chopped herbs; add lemon juice and pepper, if desired. Mix well. Shape the butter into attractive pats or pipe butter rosettes onto a baking sheet. Freeze for 2 hours. Store butter pieces in sealed plastic bags in the freezer. Herb butter will keep well for 3 to 4 months. **Hint*** Try this method with basil, chives, garlic, oregano, parsley, sage, tarragon, thyme, or a blend of any of these flavours.

Peppery Herb Butter

½ lb.	225 g	butter
2 tbsp.	30 mL	basil, finely chopped
1 tbsp.	15 mL	chopped chives
1 tbsp.	15 mL	chopped parsley
1 tbsp.	15 mL	drained pink pepper-corns, coarsely chopped

In a medium bowl, soften the butter with a wooden spoon. Add the chopped herbs and mix well. Add the peppercorns and stir to incorporate. Form the butter into attractive pats or pipe butter rosettes onto a baking sheet. Freeze for 2 hours. Store butter pieces in sealed plastic bags in the freezer. They will keep well for 3 to 4 months.

Herb Butters and Vegetables

Prepare herb butters to complement your vegetable dishes. Here's a list of the vegetables each herb butter suits best.

* **basil butter**
  corn, peas, tomatoes, beets, carrots, cauliflower

* **chive butter**
  carrots, turnip, cauliflower, cabbage

* **dill butter**
  carrots, cauliflower

* **mint butter**
  peas

* **oregano butter**
  tomatoes, peas, beans

* **parsley butter**
  zucchini, tomatoes, corn, potatoes, beans, carrots, peas, beets, cauliflower

* **tarragon butter**
  beets, cauliflower

Note ❋ Peppercorns come packed in liquid. They are soft and can be easily chopped or crushed. You can find them in the gourmet section of most large grocery stores.

Herb oil

The best herbs to use for making herb oils are basil, fennel, marjoram, mint, oregano, rosemary, sage, tarragon, and thyme. Use whole sprigs or strip the leaves and discard the stems. Use a light, good-quality oil as a base; we recommend light vegetable oils, olive oil, safflower oil, or sunflower oil.

Herb oils can have intense flavours and usually feature only a single flavour (e.g., tarragon oil, thyme oil, rosemary oil). If you want to prepare a blend, partner one herb with a complementary flavour. Combine no more than three herbs in an oil: otherwise, the flavours can grow indistinct, even muddy.

❦

If you want to serve herb butter at the table, keep the portions in ice-water until serving. Garnish the serving dish with edible flower petals or sprigs of fresh herbs.

Method 1 ❋ **Cold-infused oil**

Fill a freshly sterilized jar with a sealable lid with washed and dried herbs. Bruise the herbs lightly to release their flavours. Cover the herbs with your oil of choice and seal the jar tightly. Place the jar in a sunny windowsill for 4 weeks. Shake the jar daily. Strain the oil into a container with a pouring spout, then transfer to a freshly sterilized dark bottle. Seal tightly. Store in a cool, dark place.

Method 2 ❋ **Heat-infused oil**

Place a ceramic or glass bowl over a saucepan of simmering water. Pour 2 cups (500 mL) of the oil of your choice in the bowl. Stir in 2 cups (500 mL) fresh herbs (1 cup/250 mL dried herbs). Let the herb/oil mixture stand over low heat for 3 hours. Strain the oil into a container with a pouring spout, then transfer to a freshly sterilized dark bottle. Seal tightly. Store in a cool, dark place.

Seasoned bread crumbs

Personalize homemade bread crumbs by adding your favourite herbs. Use crumbs for breading meat and fish, binding meatloaf and hamburger, topping casseroles, and stuffing vegetables. Store homemade crumbs in plastic containers or resealable plastic bags; they will keep well for several weeks in the pantry or freezer.

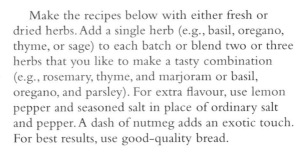

Make the recipes below with either fresh or dried herbs. Add a single herb (e.g., basil, oregano, thyme, or sage) to each batch or blend two or three herbs that you like to make a tasty combination (e.g., rosemary, thyme, and marjoram or basil, oregano, and parsley). For extra flavour, use lemon pepper and seasoned salt in place of ordinary salt and pepper. A dash of nutmeg adds an exotic touch. For best results, use good-quality bread.

A small resealable sandwich bag will hold about 3 cups of bread crumbs, which is enough to bread 4 to 6 portions of meat, fish, or poultry. After breading, discard any leftover crumbs.

Seasoned Bread Crumbs

1 loaf, sliced		white bread, crusts attached
2 tbsp.	30 mL	finely chopped fresh herbs
or		
2 tsp.	10 mL	dried herbs
½ tsp	2.5 mL	paprika
salt and pepper, to taste		

Method 1 ❋ Fresh crumbs ❋ Use bread 1 to 2 days old. Break the bread into pieces. In a food processor or blender, process the bread into crumbs in small batches. Stir in the herbs, paprika, salt, and pepper. Store in a sealed container in a cool, dry place or freeze in resealable sandwich bags. Makes about 6 cups (1500 mL) of lightly packed crumbs.

Method 2 ❋ Dry crumbs ❋ Use dry bread. Preheat oven to 200 to 250°F (100 to 110°C). Place the bread slices on a baking sheet. Bake in the oven for 30 to 40 minutes, turning once or twice, until the bread is dry but not coloured. Break bread into pieces and process into crumbs in a food processor or blender. Stir in the herbs, paprika, salt, and pepper. Store in a sealed container in a cool, dry place or freeze in resealable sandwich bags. Makes about 3½ cups (875 mL) of fine bread crumbs.

25 FAVOURITE CULINARY HERBS

lemon balm

Melissa officinalis

Semi-hardy perennial; usually grown as an
  annual in colder climates.
Height 20 to 80 cm, can reach 1.5 m; spread to 60 cm.
Loosely branched, with upright growth habit.

*My friend Joanne Grumley once planted a patch of lemon
balm, her favourite herb, in my yard. One day, she asked Dave
Grice, our long-time family friend and greenhouse manager, to till
the garden, which was getting weedy and overgrown. Dave
misunderstood and tilled the entire plot, destroying all of Joanne's
work. Well, Joanne was livid, Dave was mortified, and I had to
suppress a chuckle. My husband Ted has tilled under a few of my
crops over the years, and it was a relief to know that it didn't
just happen to me!* ❋ *As the name implies, lemon
balm has a bright, fresh lemon taste. For anyone
who loves lemons, this herb is indispensable!*

Try it!

Melissa officinalis (**common lemon balm**) is the most usual variety and
  is widely available.

The word balm is a contraction of *balsam*, traditionally considered the king of the sweet-smelling oils.

Planting

Lemon balm may be started indoors from seed or grown from young plants purchased from a garden centre.

How much ❋ At least two plants.

When ❋ Early spring; can withstand a light frost.

Where ❋ Full sun; will tolerate part shade. Gold or variegated types prefer partial shade. Prefers well-drained, sandy soil. Space plants 30 to 45 cm apart.

As the name implies, the leaves of this herb give off a strong lemon scent when crushed. It's a wonderful plant for attracting bees; in fact, the genus name for lemon balm, *Melissa*, comes from the Greek word for bees.

Care and Nurture

Lemon balm is easy to grow! Prune regularly to promote bushiness. Where lemon balm grows as a perennial, it should be divided every three to four years in the spring or fall to encourage new growth.

35

Harvesting

Leaves can be harvested throughout the growing season, until the flowers begin to bloom.

For best flavour✽ Harvest only young leaves: older leaves have a stale, musty flavour.

Leaves✽ Clip individual leaves as needed. Cut sprigs and use whole, or strip the leaves. Discard leaf stalks.

Flowers✽ Edible, but not normally eaten.

Preserving the Harvest

Lemon balm is at its best used fresh: the leaves lose their intense flavour when dried or stored. Preserve by drying.

Tips

✽ Lemon balm self-seeds and spreads easily, so you might want to grow it in a pot or isolate it in a section of your garden.

✽ Like all lemon-scented herbs, lemon balm's flavour is more intense when the plant is grown in poor soil, but the overall plant growth will be lusher in rich soil.

Lemon balm is excellent for teas—use either fresh or dried leaves.

Lemon balm may be used in aromatic herb baths. Dried leaves add a lemon scent to potpourris and herb pillows.

Cucumber and Lemon Balm Marmalade

Lovely rich lemon flavour with a definite taste of lemon balm.
—Joyce

2 cups	500 mL	finely chopped or grated cucumber (peeled and seeded)
⅓ cup	75 mL	finely chopped lemon balm
⅓ cup	75 mL	lemon juice
2 tbsp.	25 mL	lemon peel
4 cups	1 L	sugar
1 pouch	1 pouch	Certo liquid
green food colouring, if desired		

Thoroughly combine cucumber, lemon balm, lemon juice, peel, and sugar in a large saucepan. Bring to a full rolling boil and boil hard 1 minute, stirring constantly. Remove from heat and immediately stir in Certo liquid. Stir and skim for 5 minutes to prevent floating particles. Ladle quickly into hot sterilized jars, leaving ¼-inch (0.5-cm) headspace. Wipe jar rims thoroughly with a clean, wet cloth. Seal and process for 10 minutes in a boiling-water bath. Cool. Leave 24 hours, remove jar bands, wipe jars thoroughly, label, and store in a cool, dry place for up to 1 year.
Yield✳ 4 small jars.

Freeze finely chopped lemon balm leaves in ice-cube trays to add to coolers and summer drinks. Chopped leaves also make an excellent addition to salads. Whole leaves can be tucked inside the foil packet when you're barbecuing fish.

Lemon balm leaves can be crystallized and used to decorate cakes (see pages 134–35).

basil

Ocimum basilicum

Very tender annual.

Height 30 to 60 cm; spread 30 to 45 cm.

Highly aromatic branching herb that forms large,
lush mounds in the garden or container.

*Most gardeners today have at least one pot of basil
growing somewhere, whether it's on the windowsill, on
the deck, or in the garden. I was first introduced to basil in the
mid-1970s, when Italian immigrants started asking for it at
our U-pick garden. I'm so grateful they brought this
lovely, versatile herb to my attention! Now I always
keep two pots of basil growing on the kitchen
counter. ✳ One of the mainstays of herbal
cuisine, basil has a wide range of uses. It's
the perfect herb to stir into pasta sauces,
meat recipes, or almost any dish I can name. It's also one
of the few herbs whose flavour increases when cooked.*

Try these!

Ocimum basilicum 'Sweet Basil' ✳ The standard, familiar green basil;
prolific, with nice fragrance and colour

Ocimum basilicum 'Dark Opal' ✳ Nice spicy flavour and scent; leaves
deep purple and bronze

Ocimum basilicum 'Genovese' ✳ Extra-large leaves with great fragrance
and flavour; great pesto basil; originated from the Genoa area of Italy

Ocimum basilicum 'Sweet Dani' ✳ Very fragrant lemon scent, especially
when leaves are rubbed; an All-America Selections winner in 1998

Smaller varieties of basil can be used as edging for garden borders. In pots or hanging baskets, basil can serve as a foil for brightly coloured bedding plants.

Planting

Basil can be difficult to grow from seed. If you enjoy a challenge, start indoors from seed; otherwise, grow from young plants purchased from a garden centre.

How much✻ Two or three plants; plant up to ten if you intend to make pesto.

When✻ Two weeks after the date of the last average spring frost.

Where✻ Full sun, sheltered. Excellent in containers. Needs rich, well-drained soil. Space plants 30 cm apart in the garden.

Care and Nurture

Basil requires extra care to grow well. Overwatering can cause root-rot. Pinch off shoots to promote robust new growth and a bushy form. Basil tends to get woody when it gets old.

Basil makes an attractive accent plant in the garden.

Harvesting

For the most bountiful harvest, prune flowers as soon as they appear. Basil's flavour grows much stronger as the leaves age, losing much of their delicate, sweet scent.

For best flavour✳ Choose young, small, tender leaves for mild aroma and taste. Harvest mid-morning, after the dew has evaporated and before the day gets too hot.

Leaves✳ Harvest individual leaves by clipping the leaf stalk where it attaches to the plant stem. Cut sprigs and use whole, or strip the leaves. Discard tough stalks.

Flowers✳ Pick just as flowers emerge. Clip the flower stalk where it attaches to the plant stem; discard stalk.

purple basil

Preserving the Harvest

The best way to preserve basil is to freeze it: frozen basil retains nearly 100% of its essential oils. Blanch the leaves quickly in boiling water, dry them on paper towels, and freeze them in sealed plastic bags. A short-term way to preserve basil is in oil. Wash and dry the leaves and then pack them into a clean, dry glass jar. (It's important to use a glass jar, as plastic will leach out the flavour of the leaves.) Sprinkle salt over each layer of leaves, and when the jar is full, fill it with olive oil to cover the leaves. Close the jar with a tight-fitting lid and store in the refrigerator. The leaves will keep for 7 to 10 days.

African blue basil

sweet basil

Tips

* Basil seed often harbours a fungal disease called *Fusarium oxysporum*. Fusarium affects germination and causes sudden wilting of leaves; the stems turn brown, and the plant eventually topples and dies. The fungus can be caused by both contaminated seeds and soil, and spreads easily through contaminated soil and leaves. There is currently no way to control this disease, but some seed companies are attempting to eliminate fusarium from basil seed.

* Here are some other basil varieties you might like to try.
  Ocimum basilicum minimum **'Green Globe'** is a very dense, rounded basil with a uniform growth habit.
  Ocimum basilicum **'Nufar'** is a new sweet basil hybrid that has shown excellent resistance to fusarium; it's a Genovese-type basil with great fragrance and flavour.
  Ocimum sp. **'Siam Queen'** was an All-America Selections winner in 1997; it has deep-purple stems and flowers that contrast with its dark-green leaves, and its flavour is spicy with an anise-licorice scent and flavour.
  Ocimum **'African Blue'** has a different growth habit and leaf form from sweet basils: its leaves aren't as smooth and have a slight bluish tone, and the leaf veins, stems, and flowers are purple; it has an unusual flavour with a sweet camphor scent. African Blue is probably the easiest basil to grow indoors because it is not susceptible to fusarium.

* Basil is among the least frost-tolerant herbs. Around the greenhouse, we joke that you should never walk by basil with a tray of ice cubes, lest you freeze it. Shadier locations cause the plants to stretch, leaving them weak, gangly, and more susceptible to disease.

* To promote leaf growth, pick off flower shoots as they appear, unless you want to harvest a few flowers, which taste like the leaves, only milder.

* Avoid adding compost to the soil where basil is to be grown: compost tends to increase root-rot problems.

In India, basil is sacred, dedicated to the gods Vishnu and Krishna. It is commonly grown in pots near temples. Recognizing its importance in Indian culture, during the colonial era the British used it like a Bible, to swear oaths upon.

Try this soup with Herbed Focaccia (see page 146) or Chives Biscuits (see page 211).
—John

Herbed Onion and Tomato Soup

3 cups	750 mL	finely chopped onion
4	4	garlic cloves, crushed
½ cup	125 mL	olive oil
5	5	large tomatoes, peeled, seeded, and diced
3 tbsp.	45 mL	chopped fresh basil
3 tbsp.	45 mL	chopped fresh thyme
5 10-oz. cans	5 284-mL cans	chicken bouillon
or		
6 cups	1.5 L	chicken stock
salt and pepper, to taste		
chopped fresh chives and parsley		

In a large saucepan over low heat, combine olive oil, onions, and garlic. Cook, stirring occasionally, until the onions are soft, about 10 to 12 minutes. Add chopped tomatoes, basil, and thyme; cook for 3 minutes. Add the bouillon or stock over medium-high heat and bring to a boil. Lower heat and simmer for 15 minutes. Season to taste. Serve and garnish with chives and parsley.
Serving suggestions✻ This soup is also excellent with bread fried in olive oil sprinkled with fresh chives and parsley. Cut slices of baguette ½ inch (1 cm) thick and cook to golden-brown in hot olive oil. Drain bread on paper towel. Place the bread in the bottom of the bowl and pour the soup over the bread. Or try this soup with white-bread croutons! Make ¼-inch (0.5-cm) dice from white bread and fry in olive oil until golden. Drain on paper towel and serve in a bowl as a garnish for the soup.

*From northern Thailand, this
chicken and rice dish has a
sensational flavour.*
—Joyce

Thai Basil Chicken Breasts with Coconut Rice

1 or 2	1 or 2	garlic cloves, sliced
1 tsp.	5 mL	oil
4	4	skinless, boneless chicken breasts
1 cup	250 mL	basil, thinly sliced and divided
1 inch	2.5 cm	piece of ginger, shredded
2 tbsp.	25 mL	seasoned rice wine vinegar (such as Marukan)
2 tbsp.	25 mL	light soy sauce or fish sauce
¼ cup	50 mL	water
2 tsp.	10 mL	brown sugar or honey
dash	dash	pepper

Combine garlic and oil in a large frying pan or
sauté pan. Cook until garlic is golden and remove
from pan. Pat chicken thoroughly dry with paper
towels. Cook until lightly browned on each side.
Return garlic to pan with half of the basil, ginger,
vinegar, water, soy, sugar, and pepper. Cook,
covered, 6 to 8 minutes or until chicken tests
done. Watch carefully as mixture scorches easily;
add a small amount of water if necessary. Spoon
chicken onto serving dish; add remaining basil
to pan juices and pour over chicken. Serve with
steamed green beans and coconut rice. Serves 4.
Coconut Rice❋ Combine 1½ cups (375 mL)
of thoroughly washed rice (use a fragrant, long-
grain Thai variety) with 2½ cups (625 mL) good-
quality canned coconut milk (preferably packed
in Thailand) and ½ cup (125 mL) water in a
heavy pot with a tight-fitting lid. Stir, cover, and
simmer until all water is absorbed (approximately
20 to 25 minutes). Watch carefully: this rice burns
easily. Remove from heat and allow rice to sit
10 minutes. Remove cover, fluff with a fork, and
serve. Add salt if desired.

*Offer Herb Butter (page 30) on
the side—excellent!*
—John

Basil-Stuffed Steaks

5 cups	1.25 L	basil leaves, tightly packed
5 tbsp.	75 mL	olive oil
2 tsp.	10 mL	garlic powder
2 tsp.	10 mL	onion powder
6 6-oz.	6 0.18-kg	centre-cut tenderloin steaks
cracked black pepper		
salt		
wooden skewers cut in 3½-inch (8-cm) lengths		

In a medium saucepan, boil lightly salted
water. Meanwhile, rinse basil leaves in cold
water. Remove the water from heat and add
the basil leaves. Steep for 1 minute; drain
well. Gently press any excess water out of
the leaves; set leaves aside. In a small bowl,
combine olive oil, garlic powder, and onion
powder; set aside. With a sharp knife, make
a pocket in the side of each steak. Stuff the
blanched, drained basil leaves in the pockets.
Pin the steaks closed with wooden skewers.
Brush the steaks with seasoned olive oil.
Roll steaks in cracked black pepper; season
with salt. Grill or barbecue steaks, brushing
with seasoned oil while they cook, until
they reach the desired degree of doneness.

Quick cream cheese, tomato, and basil snack:
Mix chopped basil with cream cheese or chèvre.
Spread on bread, toast, focaccia, crusty bread, or
crackers. Top with tomato slices, season to taste,
and garnish with a whole basil leaf.

Make this recipe year-round by using dried herbs—use only half the amounts called for.
—John

Risotto with Italian Herbs

7 cups	1.75 L	chicken stock, broth, **or** bouillon
8 tbsp.	125 mL	butter
½ cup	125 mL	finely chopped onion
2 cups	500 mL	arborio rice
½ cup	125 mL	dry white wine
2 tbsp.	30 mL	finely chopped fresh basil
1 tbsp.	15 mL	finely chopped fresh oregano
1 tbsp.	15 mL	finely chopped fresh thyme
½ cup	125 mL	freshly grated Parmesan cheese

In a large saucepan, bring chicken stock to a boil; reduce heat to low and simmer. In a large open skillet or heavy saucepan, melt half the butter over medium heat. Add the onion to the butter and cook without browning for 7 to 8 minutes, stirring constantly. Add the rice, stirring to coat the grains with butter; cook for 1 to 2 minutes. Add the wine and continue cooking until it is almost absorbed. Add 2 cups (500 mL) of hot stock, stirring occasionally, until the liquid is absorbed. Add another 2 cups (500 mL) of stock and cook, stirring occasionally. Add the chopped herbs to 2 cups (500 mL) of hot stock and let steep for 3 to 4 minutes. Pour the stock and herbs over the rice, stir, and cook until the liquid is absorbed. Continue adding stock, ½ cup (125 mL) at a time, until the rice is soft. Stir in the remaining butter. Add the grated Parmesan and gently mix with a fork; do not mash the rice. Serve at once.

Hint ❋ Arborio rice is an Italian short-grain rice. It is a sticky rice, well suited to this recipe.

47

borage

Borago officinalis

Hardy annual; self-seeds readily.
Height 60 to 90 cm; spread to 60 cm.
Prolific species with hollow stems, hairy ovate
leaves, and blue or purple star-shaped flowers.

ob Stadnyk, our perennials manager, grew up on a farm near Rochester, Alberta. He used to grow borage to attract bees to his vegetable garden. This trick worked well, especially—strangely enough—with the cucumbers. Bob recalls raising bumper crops of cucumbers whenever borage was growing nearby! ✳ Borage is an exceptionally pretty plant, with star-shaped purple flowers and silvery-haired foliage that gives the plant a glistening, metallic sheen. The mild flavour of the leaves and flowers is similar to cucumber.

Try it!

***Borago officinalis* (common borage)** is the most usual variety
and is widely available.

Planting

Seed borage directly into the garden or, to get a jump on the season, set out young plants purchased from a garden centre.

How much At least two plants.

When After the date of the average last spring frost.

Where Full sun; will tolerate some shade. Prefers sandy, well-drained soil; will tolerate poor soil. Space plants at least 60 cm apart.

Care and Nurture

Borage is easy to grow! Although borage is drought-tolerant once the plant is established, young plants need lots of water.

Harvesting

Fresh borage leaves can be harvested continuously, like spinach. The flowers grow in clusters called racemes; harvest individual flowers rather than the whole raceme.

For best flavour Remove the pistils and stamens (the black centre) before you eat the flowers.

Leaves Harvest as needed by cutting from the stem.

Flowers Harvest as they open. Clip the flower stalk where it attaches to the plant stem; discard stalk.

Preserving the Harvest

Use only fresh borage leaves—they do not store well. Borage flowers can be frozen in ice-cubes.

Tips

Borage flowers are attractive and tasty.

* Any vegetable crop that needs pollination—squash, cucumbers, and the like—will benefit greatly from a nearby borage plant, because borage flowers are a favourite of bees.

* If you choose to grow borage in a container, choose a large pot. The plants grow rapidly and need lots of room. Half whiskey-barrels are perfect.

* Borage looks much more attractive when it's grown with other plants. Use it as a feature plant with other culinary herbs surrounding it.

One of those quick and
delicious summer recipes
that we all love to prepare!
—Joyce

Cheesecake Tart with Raspberries and Borage

¾ cup	175 mL	sugar
2		large eggs
1½ tsp.	7 mL	pure vanilla extract
1 tsp.	1 mL	lemon **or** orange peel
½ cup	125 mL	top-quality biscuit mix
2 8-oz. packages	2 250-g packages	cream cheese, cubed, at room temperature

Topping		
1 cup	250 mL	sour cream
2 tbsp.	25 mL	sugar
½ tsp.	2 mL	vanilla
2 tbsp.	25 mL	borage petals

fresh raspberries		
red currant **or** crabapple jelly		
borage blossoms		

In a blender or food processor, combine the sugar, eggs, vanilla, peel, biscuit mix, and cream cheese. Blend on low and then high speed until rich and creamy, approximately 3 minutes. Pour into a well-greased 8–9 inch (20–23 cm) French tart pan or cake pan. Bake at 350°F (175°C) for 30 minutes or until slightly puffed and golden. Remove from oven. Combine topping ingredients and spread over hot tart. Chill for at least 3 hours. To serve, cover liberally with raspberries. Brush lightly with melted jelly and decorate with borage blossoms (see note on flower preparation, page 24). Offer whipped cream on the side if you wish.

*Blue borage flowers make a lovely
edible garnish for this soup.*
—John

Cold Cucumber
Soup with Borage

5	5	small English cucumbers
1 cup	250 mL	1% milk
½ cup	125 mL	plain low-fat yogourt
1 tbsp.	15 mL	lime juice
1 tbsp.	15 mL	borage leaves, chopped
1 tbsp.	15 mL	diced yellow **or** red pepper

Peel, seed, and chop 4 cucumbers. In a
food processor with a steel blade, purée
the cucumbers until smooth. Add the milk
and yogourt; blend well for 30 seconds.
Transfer mixture to a large bowl. Stir in
the lime juice. Cut the remaining cucumber
into small dice. Add diced cucumber and
borage leaves to the purée; stir well to
combine. Cover bowl with plastic wrap
and refrigerate 2 to 3 hours. Serve in chilled
bowls, garnished with diced peppers.

Serve cantaloupe and ice cream
topped with borage flowers.

Add chopped borage leaves and flowers
to summer drinks like lemonade or iced tea.
Borage is fantastic chopped up in salads and
cream cheese, and also goes well with nasturtiums.

chives

Allium schoenoprasum

Hardy perennial.

Height 20 to 60 cm; spread 30 to 40 cm.

Grows in clumps of long, cylindrical, hollow
  leaves, with globe-shaped clusters of
  pale-purple to pink flowers atop tall,
  slender stalks.

I've eaten chives for as long as I can remember.

When I was a little girl, it seemed that everyone

grew them in their backyards, close to the kitchen

door. Chives are small, yet they have one of the

finest flavours of the onion family—which includes

stiff competition like garlic, leeks, and shallots.

* *Chives are extremely versatile and easy to grow.*

They can be grown indoors or out, in small or large pots,

and they positively thrive in the garden. They are decorative,

inexpensive, hardy, low maintenance, practically immune to

pests, and tasty. What more can we ask from a plant?

Try these!

***Allium schoenoprasum* (common chives)** * Good for growing indoors;
  excellent flavour from dark-green leaves

***Allium schoenoprasum* 'Grolau' (windowsill chives)** * Great onion/
  garlic flavour, with white flowers

***Allium tuberosum* (garlic chives/Japanese chives)** * Flat-leaf variety
  from Japan

Planting

As with all perennials, choose your location carefully, because chives come back year after year; however, they are not invasive. Although chives can be started from seed, most people start with clumps of young plants purchased from a garden centre or split the roots from an established plant.

How much✻ One clump (six to ten bulbs).

When✻ As soon as the ground can be worked; very tolerant of cold and frost.

Where✻ Partial sun to shade. Prefers rich, well-drained soil. Space clumps 30 to 45 cm apart.

Care and Nurture

Chives are easy to grow! For large, mild chives, water often; for smaller, more intensely flavoured chives, don't water as frequently. (Newly planted clumps need to be watered regularly.) Divide old clumps or plant in a new spot in your garden every 3 years to prevent crowding and maintain plant vigour.

Chives were recorded in Chinese literature 4000 years ago and were eaten by Marco Polo on his journeys to the Far East. In Europe, chives were not generally appreciated and widely cultivated until the Middle Ages.

Chives make a great perennial border. The blossoms can also be used as cut-flowers.

A clump of chives makes an attractive addition to mixed flower beds.

Chives add great flavour to salads.

Harvesting

Harvest chives throughout the growing season, using clean scissors.

For best flavour✳ Harvest mid-morning, after the dew has evaporated and before the day gets too hot.

Leaves✳ Harvest as needed by trimming individual leaves a few centimetres above the ground.

Flowers✳ Harvest when fully open but before the colours begin to fade. Cut growing stem a few centimetres above the ground; clip flower head and discard stem.

Preserving the Harvest

Chives are best used fresh and are fairly easy to grow indoors if you want a year-round supply. They are best preserved by freezing, either whole or chopped. Chives do not retain their flavour well when dried in the home.

Tips

✳ To keep fresh chives available through winter, here's a trick you may want to try. In late summer, take a clump of chives and transplant them into a good-sized pot. Sink the container into the ground, then remove after the first hard frost has killed the tops. Trim the dead material and keep the pot in a cool spot in your house (such as a cold room) for about 3 months. After this period of dormancy, place the container on a sunny windowsill and keep it watered. New growth should appear in a few weeks. Harvest as needed.

✳ Many people ask me, "what's the difference between chives and green onions? Can I use them the same way?" While both plants are members of the *Allium* family, chives lack the fleshy, bulbous base of green onions (or other onions, for that matter). The flavour of chives is also subtler than that of green onions.

Samosas
(Savoury Turnovers)

Once you've tried the basic form of these delicious pastries, you can experiment by adding small amounts of other herbs and finely chopped vegetables to the filling.
—John

3 cups	750 mL	flour
¼ cup	50 mL	clarified butter, melted
pinch		salt
¾ cup	175 mL	cold water (approx.)
1 tbsp.	15 mL	vegetable oil
3 tbsp.	45 mL	chives
1	1	medium onion, diced
1 tsp.	5 mL	ginger root, peeled and grated
½ tsp.	2.5 mL	curry powder
4	4	medium potatoes, cooked and diced
1½ cups	375 mL	frozen peas, thawed
1 tsp.	5 mL	coriander
salt and pepper, to taste		
oil for deep-frying		

In a large bowl, combine flour, butter, and salt.
Add enough water to form a smooth dough (there
should be no loose particles left in the bowl). Knead
dough, allow to rest, covered, for 3 to 4 minutes,
and then rest in the refrigerator, still covered, for
1 hour. In a skillet, heat the oil over medium heat.
Add the chives, onion, ginger, and curry powder;
cook 3 to 4 minutes. Add the potatoes and peas.
Cook, stirring occasionally, until the potatoes are
heated through. Season with coriander, salt, and
pepper. Cool. Form the rested dough into 12 small
pieces. With a rolling pin, flatten each piece into a
4-inch (10-cm) circle. Fold each circle in half. Roll
the semi-circle to form a thin layer of dough. Place
a portion of filling on the dough. Fold the corners
of the dough over the filling to form a triangle.
Moisten the edges of the dough with water and
pinch to seal. When all the samosas are sealed, heat
the oil to 350°F (180°C). Deep-fry samosas until
golden-brown. Remove with a skimmer or tongs
and drain on paper towels. Serve hot or cold with
dipping sauce.

These muffins are great with Herb Butter (page 30).
—John

Potato Muffins

2	2	large egg yolks, beaten
2½ cups	625 mL	finely grated potato
3 tbsp.	45 mL	grated onion
½ cup	125 mL	all-purpose flour
1 tsp.	5 mL	baking powder
¼ cup	60 mL	melted butter
1 tbsp.	15 mL	finely chopped chives
salt and white pepper, to taste		
3	3	egg whites
pinch	pinch	salt

Grease 10 medium muffin cups. Preheat oven to 400°F (200°C). In a large bowl, combine the beaten egg yolks, grated potatoes, grated onion, flour, baking powder, melted butter, chives, salt, and pepper. In a medium bowl, beat the egg whites with a pinch of salt until they hold stiff peaks. Fold the beaten egg whites into the potato mixture. Fill the prepared muffin cups two-thirds full. Bake for 20 to 25 minutes or until the muffins are golden-brown.

How to Make Clarified Butter

Cut 1 lb. (454 g) of butter into small pieces. Place butter in top pan of a double boiler and heat until the butter is completely melted. Do not stir. Remove from heat. Skim any residue from the top of the butter and discard. With a small ladle or spoon, skim the oil carefully and transfer to a clean container. Leave any residue (buttermilk and salt) in the double boiler; discard. The clarified butter will keep well in the refrigerator.

Mashed Potatoes
with Chives and Sour Cream

3 lbs.	1.4 kg	peeled potatoes, cut into equal-sized pieces
¼ cup	65 mL	light cream
2 tbsp.	30 mL	butter
pinch	pinch	nutmeg
salt and white pepper, to taste		
1 cup	250 mL	sour cream
4 tbsp.	60 mL	chopped fresh chives

Try this recipe with dill in place of the chives. Use only half the amount called for, because dill is a strong-tasting herb.
—John

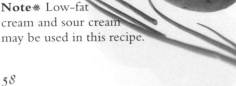

Garlic chives have a wonderful garlicky flavour. I love them in salads, where the garlic taste complements the other flavours beautifully.

In a large saucepan, boil the potatoes with water and a pinch of salt; cook uncovered for 15 to 20 minutes or until tender. Drain potatoes well in a colander. Return the drained potatoes to the saucepan; cover with a lid. Heat the cream and butter in a small saucepan over medium-high heat. Season the potatoes with nutmeg, salt, and pepper. With an electric mixer, mash the potatoes, adding the heated cream and butter. Mix until the potatoes are smooth and light. Add ½ cup (125 mL) of sour cream and 2 tbsp. (30 mL) of chopped chives; mix well. In a small bowl, mix the remaining sour cream and chives. Place the potatoes in an ovenproof casserole dish. Spread the sour cream–chives mixture over the potatoes; bake at 325°F (160°C) for 10 to 15 minutes. Serve hot.
Note✳ Low-fat cream and sour cream may be used in this recipe.

Other herbs may be added to this recipe. Try 1 tbsp. (15 mL) of finely chopped basil, thyme, parsley, or oregano.
—John

Salmon with Mustard and Chives

4 6-oz.	4 180-g	salmon steaks
salt and ground black pepper, to taste		
1½ cups	375 mL	cereal cream, cold
1 cup	250 mL	fish stock
½ cup	125 mL	dry white wine
sachet of 2 cloves, 1 bay leaf, 2 sprigs thyme, and 3 sprigs parsley		
1 tbsp.	15 mL	grainy mustard
3 tbsp.	45 mL	chopped fresh chives
2 tsp.	10 mL	lemon juice

Chop a small amount of chives and add to a simple mayonnaise or tartar sauce for a nice variation.

Season the salmon with salt and pepper. In a medium-sized bowl, combine the cream, fish stock, and white wine. Place fish steaks in a skillet and pour the liquid over the fish. Add sachet and bring the liquid to a simmer over medium heat. Reduce the heat to low and simmer gently for 10 to 12 minutes. Remove fish and keep warm. Remove sachet. Increase heat to medium-high and reduce sauce to 1 cup. Check seasoning. Stir in mustard, chives, and lemon juice. Pour the sauce over the fish and serve immediately.

Note ❋ Light cream may be used in place of cereal cream.

Hint ❋ I use cheesecloth for making sachets; a tea ball also works well.

cilantro (coriander)

Coriandrum sativum

Tender annual.
Height 30 to 60 cm; spread 10 to 45 cm.
Erect-growing herb with strongly scented,
   lobe-shaped leaves.

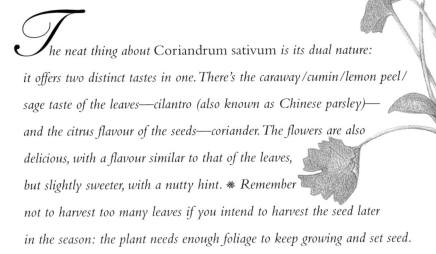

The neat thing about Coriandrum sativum *is its dual nature:
it offers two distinct tastes in one. There's the caraway/cumin/lemon peel/
sage taste of the leaves—cilantro (also known as Chinese parsley)—
and the citrus flavour of the seeds—coriander. The flowers are also
delicious, with a flavour similar to that of the leaves,
but slightly sweeter, with a nutty hint.* ❋ *Remember
not to harvest too many leaves if you intend to harvest the seed later
in the season: the plant needs enough foliage to keep growing and set seed.*

Try it!

***Coriandrum sativum* (cilantro, leaf coriander, Chinese parsley)** is the
   most usual variety and is widely available; the flavour is similar to a blend
   of parsley and citrus.

Planting

Seed cilantro directly into the garden or, to get a jump on the season, set out young plants purchased from a garden centre.

How much✽ Two or three plants.

When✽ After all danger of frost has passed.

Where✽ Full sun, sheltered. Prefers light, well-drained soil with low nitrogen content. Space plants 25 to 30 cm apart and rows 75 cm apart.

Care and Nurture

Cilantro is easy to grow! For best leaf development, try to keep cilantro from flowering. Coriander is quick to produce seed, bolting when temperatures reach 21° C.

Harvesting

If you've ever grown cilantro, you know that picking off the flower buds can be a full-time job. Fortunately, the flowers taste wonderful—their flavour is similar to that of the leaves, but slightly sweeter.

For best flavour✽ Choose lower leaves, which are broader and more flavourful than younger, upper leaves, which have a milder taste and a pungent aroma.

Leaves✽ Harvest throughout the growing season. Cut sprigs and use whole, or trim the leaflets. Tender stems can be eaten, but discard tough older stems.

Flowers✽ Pick as they appear, just after they have opened. Clip the flower stalk where it attaches to the plant stem; use stalk and all.

Seeds✽ Collect as soon as they ripen (harden and turn brown), late in the season.

cilantro flowers

61

For generations, British children have been rewarded with "comfits." These sugar-coated pink or white candies withstood sucking for a long time. When the sugar coating was gone, what remained in the middle was a coriander seed. Coriander seed is also found in the middle of jawbreakers.

Preserving the Harvest

Store fresh cilantro stem down in a glass of water; cover the leaves with a plastic bag. Change the water every two days. The leaves will keep for up to a week. Cilantro leaves do not dry well but may be frozen or preserved in light oil. Cilantro flowers may be used fresh or preserved in oil, butter, or vinegar. Coriander seed is used dried.

Tips

* Cilantro is one herb most gardeners can sow directly into the garden. Sow cilantro when you sow your carrots and don't thin the plants. The result will be numerous fine, small plants with lots of beautiful green leaves.

The best known part of cilantro is the seed (coriander), which is a major ingredient of curry powder.

The quality of coriander's volatile oils increases in northern regions. Oil yield increases during cool, moist summers. The optimum growing temperature for coriander is 18°C.

Raw coriander seed is a good breath freshener.

In the language of flowers,
coriander means "hidden worth."

*Experiment with
different varieties of mint
to discover new tastes!*
—John

Scallops Ceviche with Herbed Vinaigrette

1 lb.	450 g	scallops
2 tsp.	10 mL	chopped cilantro
1 tsp.	5 mL	chopped mint
1 tsp.	5 mL	mustard seed
½ cup	125 mL	lime juice
salt and ground black pepper, to taste		
½	½	honeydew melon
Dressing		
1 tbsp.	15 mL	dill-flavoured **or** apple-cider vinegar
½ tsp.	2.5 mL	sugar
2 tbsp.	30 mL	vegetable oil

Cut the scallops into small pieces and place
them in a ceramic bowl. Add the cilantro,
mint, mustard seed, and lime juice; mix well.
Season with salt and pepper. Cover bowl
and marinate scallops for 6 to 8 hours,
stirring occasionally (the lime juice will
"cook" the scallops). Make small melon
balls from the honeydew; refrigerate. Make
the dressing by whisking the oil slowly into
the vinegar and sugar. Just before serving,
mix the melon balls with the scallops and
add the dressing. Serve in chilled glasses
or on a bed of mixed greens.

Variation ❈ Cantaloupe may be used
in place of the honeydew melon.

Hint ❈ Use fresh seafood if available, but
frozen scallops will work. Frozen scallops
tend to pick up a lot of moisture after
freezing and thawing; but if you drain
them well and let them rest on a double
layer of paper towel, most of the excess
moisture will be absorbed.

Cilantro is reputedly the world's most widely used
herb, featured prominently in the cuisines of
Mexico, the Caribbean, the Orient, and India.

Satays

⅔ cup	150 mL	chopped onion
½ cup	125 mL	soy sauce
4	4	garlic cloves, crushed
1 tbsp.	15 mL	lime juice
1 tsp.	5 mL	galangal powder
2 tbsp.	30 mL	cilantro leaves
cumin, turmeric, and black pepper, to taste		
1 lb.	454 g	lean pork, cubed
or		
1 lb.	454 g	boneless, skinless chicken breasts, sliced into thin strips
or		
1 lb.	454 g	boneless flank steak, sliced into thin strips

In food processor with the blade attachment, combine the chopped onion, soy sauce, garlic, lime juice, galangal powder, and cilantro. Season with cumin, turmeric, and black pepper. Place the meat in a ceramic or glass bowl. Add the purée; mix well. Cover and marinate for 4 to 6 hours at room temperature. Remove the meat from the marinade and thread onto wooden skewers (soak skewers for 30 minutes first to prevent burning). Grill or barbecue the meat for 10 to 12 minutes, turning frequently, until the meat is browned on all sides.

Hint ❋ Galangal powder is found in the Oriental section of most major grocery stores or any Vietnamese grocery store. It is made from a ground, dried root. You can substitute ginger for galangal powder, as its flavour is similar.

65

Backyard Steak with Bloody Mary Sauce

4 8-oz.	4 0.25-kg	sirloin **or** rib steaks
1 tsp.	5 mL	coriander seed, crushed
1	1	garlic clove, crushed
2 tbsp.	25 mL	oil
2 tbsp.	25 mL	aged balsamic vinegar
2 tbsp.	15 mL	Worcestershire sauce

A hearty steak with a dipping sauce! Make extra sauce and keep it in the freezer—it's excellent for dipping hot roast beef sandwiches and rich grilled cheese sandwiches.
—Joyce

Prick steaks lightly with a fork. Combine remaining ingredients in a plastic bag. Add steaks and close bag tightly around steak. Refrigerate for only 1 to 2 hours, as this is a strong marinade and you do not want to "cook" the steak with the acid, thereby giving it a soggy texture. Remove steaks from marinade and pat them thoroughly dry with paper towels. Broil or barbecue to desired doneness, preferably crusty on the outside with a very pink interior. Serve with Bloody Mary Sauce (opposite), roasted garlic potatoes or corn on the cob, and a green salad.

An exotic Indian flavour is easily achieved by roasting chunks of potato with oil and lots of ground coriander and pepper. Garnish with finely chopped cilantro.

Bloody Mary Sauce

6	6	large very ripe tomatoes
or		
1 14-oz. can	1 398-mL can	plum tomatoes
1	1	small onion, chopped
¼ cup	50 mL	fresh cilantro, chopped
½ cup	125 mL	beef broth
or		
½ cup	125 mL	water and a beef bouillon cube
1 tbsp.	15 mL	Worcestershire sauce
2 tbsp.	25 mL	butter
2 tbsp.	25 mL	brown sugar
1 tbsp.	15 mL	fresh lemon **or** lime juice
¼ cup	50 mL	vodka

Skin, seed, and chop tomatoes. Combine with remaining ingredients except lemon/lime juice and vodka. Cook gently for 15 minutes. Remove from heat and purée. Add lemon/lime juice and vodka. Refrigerate. Warm and serve in small individual pots. May be refrigerated for up to 3 days.

Coriander is often an ingredient in the Indian spice-mixture *garam masala*. Coriander is also used as a seasoning on roast pork, lamb, and many spicy meat dishes from North Africa.

dill

Anethum graveolens

Annual; often self-seeds.

Height 60 to 90 cm; spread to 15 cm.

Tall-growing green shoots sport umbels of bright-yellow inflorescences and finely fern-like, fragrant leaves.

The scent of a lush stand of dill is one of my great gardening pleasures. I love to breathe in the remarkable aroma, a heady blend of mint, citrus, and fennel, with a hint of sea air. ✻ Like many gardeners, I use dill for pickling. Every year, my daughter-in-law Valerie and I pickle 100 to 150 jars of cucumbers, beans, and carrots. Some of my favourite memories involve this late-summer ritual. However, I use dill for more than just pickles. New potatoes, for instance, taste heavenly with dill. I also include dill in green salads and cream-cheese dip for fresh vegetables. And who hasn't enjoyed fish with fresh dill?

Try these!

***Anethum graveolens* (common dill)** ✻ Tall-growing, leafy plant with finely cut foliage

***Anethum graveolens* var. 'Fernleaf' (fernleaf dill)** ✻ More compact than common dill, with excellent leaf production; good choice for containers

Planting

Dill grows best seeded directly into the garden: it dislikes transplanting. Plant a small amount in early spring for salads and new potatoes, and several additional sowings every 2 to 3 weeks through June and early July for pickles. Sow seed thickly, as you would carrots.

How much✻ A 30-cm row for early harvest; a 3-m row for each later planting.

When✻ Around the date of the average last spring frost.

Where✻ Full sun; sheltered. Prefers rich, well-drained soil; will tolerate poor soil. Space rows 60 cm apart.

Care and Nurture

Dill is easy to grow! Once sown, garden dill requires little care other than watering if the summer is particularly dry. Dill grown in containers requires more care. Consistent watering and pruning will promote lush, leafy growth all summer long. Aphids tend to attack dill once it sets seed.

Many people tell me to avoid planting dill near fennel, because the flavour of both plants will be compromised if the two cross-pollinate. I've never had this problem, but I figure, why take a chance?

Harvesting

You can begin harvesting dill when it is only a few centimetres high. The leaves, stems, flower heads, and seeds are all edible.

For best flavour❋ Harvest whole plant just as the flowers are opening.

Leaves❋ Harvest as needed throughout the growing season. Clip sprigs where they attach to the main growing stem or cut the whole plant a few centimetres above the ground. Discard thick, tough stems.

Flowers❋ Pick complete flower heads when they turn yellow, but before they get old. Cut the stalks of the flower heads where they attach to the growing stem.

Seeds❋ Harvest seeds when flower heads turn brown; ripe seeds will fall off easily when touched.

In the Talmud, it is noted that dill was subject to a tithe, suggesting the economic importance of the herb in the ancient world.

Preserving the Harvest

Use fresh if possible. Freezing is the best way to preserve dill's flavour. Cut the whole plant before it flowers. Rinse the stems quickly, then shake and pat dry; discard any large, coarse stems. Mince with a sharp knife and freeze in a screw-top jar. Another method is to freeze the unchopped stems on a baking sheet, then transfer to resealable plastic freezer bags and return to the freezer. Dill will also keep in the fridge for a few days. Collect dill seeds and store in a clean jar with a tight-fitting lid; the seeds must be fully dried when harvested.

Seed output will decrease if summer temperatures are very high; however, oil yields increase with greater day length and heat.

Dill is a tall-growing herb, often well over 1 m tall.

Tips

* Dill can be sown quite early, so I always plant it as soon as I can get into the garden. But I hold off planting my major crop until mid-June so that it ripens at the same time as my cucumbers. This timing makes pickling much easier. The dill hasn't set seed at this point, and I prefer to use the lush, ferny growth before the flower heads mature.

* Dill readily self-sows. The seed usually survives the winter and volunteer plants spring up the following season. However, volunteer dill usually matures too early for pickling and it's particularly prone to aphids because it matures when the aphids are at their peak, so use volunteer dill when it's still very young for salads and seasoning.

* Here's an easy way to collect dill seeds! Cut stems when the seeds are nearly ripe, then tie a paper bag over the flower heads; hang upside down in bunches. The seeds will drop directly into the bag.

* For a stronger dill flavour when making pickles, stuff the entire plant into the pickling jars.

The Romans believed that dill was a "fortifying" herb, so it was common practice for gladiators heading into the arena to cover their (possibly last) meals with the herb to bolster their strength. The Romans were probably responsible for carrying dill to many of the regions where it now grows.

Serve hot with dilled sour cream or cold with Savory Mayonnaise (see page 166).
—John

Salmon Pastries in Phyllo

7.5-oz. can	213-g can	red sockeye salmon, drained and bones removed
½ cup	125 mL	chopped fresh dill
2 tbsp.	30 mL	melted butter
2 tbsp.	30 mL	lemon juice
2 tbsp.	30 mL	Dijon mustard
salt and ground black pepper, to taste		
⅓ cup	85 mL	butter
4 sheets	4 sheets	phyllo pastry
8	8	large fresh basil leaves
or		
4	4	sprigs of dill

In a medium bowl, combine the salmon, chopped dill, melted butter, lemon juice, mustard, salt, and pepper. Refrigerate. Melt the ⅓ cup (85 mL) of butter. On a flat surface, lay out 1 sheet of phyllo pastry and, using a pastry brush, lightly cover with melted butter. Place a sprig of dill or 2 basil leaves in the centre of each quarter of the sheet. Lay another single sheet on top of the leaves and press lightly. Brush this sheet lightly with melted butter. Layer the remaining 2 sheets, brushing each one lightly with melted butter. Place one quarter of the salmon mixture on each quarter of the pastry. Using a sharp knife, cut the dough into 4 rectangles. Fold the corners of each rectangle into the centre, encasing the filling; seal. Turn each rectangle upside down onto a baking sheet; brush the tops with melted butter. Bake for 20 to 25 minutes at 425°F (220°C) or until the pastries are golden-brown.

Variation❉ Pink salmon or tuna may be used in place of red sockeye salmon.

A new twist on a traditional combination.
—John

Potatoes in Herbed Sour Cream Sauce

2 lb.	1 kg	baby reds **or** new potatoes
pinch	pinch	salt
sprig	sprig	dill **or** thyme (optional)
6 tbsp.	90 mL	butter
½ cup	125 mL	sour cream
1 tbsp.	15 mL	minced thyme
1 tbsp.	15 mL	minced dill
salt and ground black pepper, to taste		
3 tbsp.	45 mL	minced parsley

Wash and scrub the potatoes. In a large saucepan, cover the potatoes with water; add a pinch of salt. (Optional: add a sprig of dill or thyme to the cooking water.) Cook the potatoes 15 to 20 minutes or until they are tender; don't overcook. Drain the potatoes well and transfer to a large bowl; set aside but keep warm. (Discard sprig of dill or thyme if used.) Melt the butter in a small saucepan over medium-low heat. Whisk in the sour cream; add the thyme and dill. Season with salt and pepper. Toss the potatoes with the herb mixture until they are coated. Sprinkle with chopped parsley and serve.

Add finely chopped baby dill to green salads, or combine chopped dill with cucumbers, vinegar, and sugar to make a simple summer salad.

Dill is an excellent addition to a simple macaroni-and-cheese casserole.

73

Delicious for lunch, or omit the
shrimp and serve as a side salad.
—Joyce

Summer Green Salad with Shrimp and Dill

2 quarts	2 L	mixed baby greens **or** a combination of leaf lettuce, spinach, romaine, and tiny nasturtium leaves
1	1	cucumber, sliced
2	2	large stalks celery, sliced
1 cup	250 mL	green seedless grapes
2 cups	500 mL	cooked baby shrimp
2 tbsp.	25 mL	chopped fresh dill
⅓ cup	75 mL	oil
2 tbsp.	25 mL	fresh lemon juice
½ tsp.	2 mL	finely grated lemon peel
1 tsp.	5 mL	sugar
½ tsp.	2 mL	salt
freshly ground black pepper, to taste		
herbed croutons		
begonias **or** borage spray		
dill sprigs		

Combine lettuce, cucumber, celery, grapes, shrimp, and dill in a clear glass bowl. Cover with plastic wrap and refrigerate up to 1 hour. Whisk together oil, lemon juice, lemon peel, sugar, salt, and pepper. Leave at room temperature until required. To serve, toss salad with dressing. Top with croutons and garnish with flowers and sprigs of dill. Serves 4 as a main course. Serve with hot creamy cheese garlic bread (opposite).

Creamy Cheese Garlic Bread

1	1	very crusty French baguette
1 to 2	1 to 2	garlic cloves, crushed
freshly ground black pepper		
dash	dash	Worcestershire sauce
1 cup	250 mL	top-quality salad dressing **or** mayonnaise
½ cup	125 mL	**each** finely grated Monterey Jack cheese **and** Parmesan cheese
1 tbsp.	25 mL	finely chopped dill

In Romania, Turkey, and Greece, dill is added to stuffed grape leaves. The Russian dish *kulebakia*—a pastry-wrapped loaf of salmon, sturgeon marrow, mushrooms, hard-boiled eggs, and lots of dill— was adopted by the French and called *coulibiac*. The Swedish dish *gravlax* is salmon cured with dill, salt, sugar, and peppercorns.

Slice baguette and place on wire rack to dry slightly (3 to 4 hours). This prevents the soggy garlic bread that is so often served! Combine remaining ingredients and refrigerate. Just before serving, spread cheese mixture thickly on French bread slices. Bake at 350°F (175°C) for 5 to 8 minutes or until cheese is melted. Serve immediately.

fennel

Foeniculum vulgare

Tender perennial.

Height 1.5 to 2 m; spread 30 to 45 cm.

An attractive plant with erect, hollow stems topped by umbels
of tiny yellow flowers and bearing feathery, light-green,
anise-scented leaves.

*I*f you like black licorice, you'll

love fennel. Fennel is closely

related to dill and has the same tall, branching

growth habit. But its taste and scent are dramatically

different. ❋ There is often confusion between the

two kinds of fennel. Common fennel is a perennial herb grown for its

feathery foliage and yellow flowers. Florence fennel is an unusual vegetable

grown for its swollen stem base. The foliage can substitute for common

fennel, but don't harvest too many leaves if you want the bulb to flesh out.

Florence fennel needs a long, warm summer to develop its bulb, and any

stress or interruption can cause it to go to seed without producing a bulb.

Try these!

Foeniculum vulgare var. *dulce* (sweet fennel)❋ Produces oval-shaped,
greenish brown seeds

Foeniculum vulgare var. *dulce* 'purpureum' (bronze fennel)❋ Produces
showy purple foliage

Foeniculum vulgare var. *azoricum* (Florence fennel, finocchio)❋ Bulb-
forming variety

Planting

Seed common fennel directly into the garden or, to get a jump on the season, set out young plants purchased from a garden centre. Florence fennel must be grown from young plants.

How much At least two plants.

When After all danger of frost has passed.

Where Full sun; common fennel will tolerate a bit of shade. Sheltered. Both prefer rich, well-drained sandy soil. Space plants 15 cm apart.

Care and Nurture

Common fennel is easy to grow! It needs little care other than watering when dry. Florence fennel should be watered when dry; when the basal bulb is about the size of a golf ball, mound the soil around the base. Continue to do this on a regular basis until the bulb is the size of a tennis ball (generally through to the end of August).

Harvesting

All parts of the fennel plant can be harvested for culinary use.

For best flavour Use leaves before flowers are fully open.

Leaves Harvest as needed throughout the growing season. Clip sprigs where they attach to the main growing stem or cut the whole plant a few centimetres above the ground. Discard thick, tough stems.

Flowers Pick complete flower heads when they turn yellow, but before they get old. Cut the stalks of the flower heads where they attach to the growing stem.

Seeds Harvest seeds when flower heads turn brown; ripe seeds will fall off easily when touched. Fennel seeds can be collected like dill seeds (see tip, page 71).

bronze fennel

Bulb (Florence fennel only) Harvest in late summer or early fall by cutting base at soil level with a sharp knife.

Preserving the Harvest

Fennel is best used fresh, although it can be frozen in the same manner as dill. The flowers are best used fresh. Keep seeds in a cool dry place. Fennel bulbs should be used fresh; they can be stored in the refrigerator for a few days.

*Beet tops or radicchio may be used
in place of Swiss chard.*
—John

Sautéed Fennel, Swiss Chard, and Pine Nuts

2 tbsp.	30 mL	olive oil
2 tbsp.	30 mL	pine nuts
3	3	cloves garlic, crushed
1	1	florence fennel bulb, trimmed and cut into ¼-inch (0.5-cm) dice
2 tbsp.	30 mL	lemon juice
1	1	large bunch Swiss chard, shredded (discard tough stems)
¼ cup	60 mL	water
salt and ground black pepper, to taste		
1	1	lemon, cut into wedges

In a large skillet or wok over medium–high heat, combine the olive oil and pine nuts; sauté until golden-brown, stirring constantly. Remove pine nuts with a slotted spoon; set aside. In the same pan, cook the crushed garlic; reduce heat to medium. Don't burn the garlic. Add the diced fennel, stirring constantly until it begins to brown. Add lemon juice; cook for 3 minutes. Add the shredded Swiss chard and water; stir to mix all ingredients. Season with salt and pepper. Cook for 5 to 7 minutes, or until the chard is wilted and tender. Remove from pan with a slotted spoon and place in serving dish; garnish with the pine nuts. Serve lemon wedges on the side.

Fennel seeds are used in desserts, breads, cakes, savoury biscuits, sauces, and beverages. They can also be used to flavour the water for poaching fish.

*For a heartier soup,
add some frozen tortellini.*
—Joyce

Garden Soup with Beans and Fennel

3	3	carrots
3	3	celery stalks
1	1	small zucchini
1	1	large onion (**or** several green onions)
1	1	small green pepper
4	4	very ripe tomatoes
or		
1 14-oz. can	1 398-mL can	diced tomatoes
1 cup	250 mL	green **or** yellow beans
1	1	garlic clove, crushed
1 19-oz. can	1 540-mL can	mixed black **or** kidney beans, rinsed and drained
3 packets or cubes chicken bouillon		
1 to 2 tbsp.	15 to 25 mL	chopped fennel
1 tbsp.	15 mL	chopped basil
lots of chopped parsley		
a few sprigs of thyme		
salt and lemon pepper, to taste		

Slice or chop all vegetables and cook in a small amount of water in a covered saucepan for 10 minutes. Add all remaining ingredients and additional water to make a soup-stew consistency. Season with salt and lemon pepper; simmer gently for another 10 minutes. Serve with grilled cheese sandwiches or rye crisp and cheese. Serves 6.

Try stuffing mackerel with fresh fennel leaves; fennel is excellent with oily fish. Fennel leaves can also be finely chopped and used in salads, sprinkled on vegetables, added to sauces, and used as garnishes.

79

The popularity of Florence fennel is on the rise. You can find it in the produce section of major grocery stores.
—John

🌿

Fennel seeds are excellent sprinkled on top of fresh apple pies prior to baking. Or add fennel seeds to fresh bread crumbs and sprinkle over a seafood casserole.

Fennel Salad with Apple and Orange Dressing

1½ to 2 lbs.	680 to 900 g	florence fennel bulbs (approx. 2)
1 tbsp.	15 mL	capers, drained
1 tbsp.	15 mL	lemon balm, chopped
1	1	golden delicious apple, cut into small dice

Dressing		
6	6	orange segments
1 tbsp.	15 mL	tarragon vinegar
1 tbsp.	15 mL	prepared mustard
2 tsp.	15 mL	sugar
4 tbsp.	90 mL	olive oil
salt and freshly ground black pepper, to taste		

Trim the tops from the fennel bulb and remove any discoloured outside leaves. Cut the trimmed bulb in half; with the flat side on the cutting surface, slice the fennel crosswise into very thin slices. Place the slices in a large bowl. Add the capers, lemon balm, and diced apples; mix well. In a food processor, blend the orange segments, mustard, vinegar, and sugar. With the motor running on low speed, add the olive oil in a slow stream. Pour the dressing over the fennel and toss together to mix well. Season to taste.

Grillade au Fenouille, a Provençal recipe, includes sea bass, red mullet, or sometimes trout. The fish are grilled, then flamed in brandy on a bed of dried fennel that burns and gives the fish a unique flavour.

hops

Humulus lupulus

Hardy perennial.

Height 3 to 6 m; spread 1.2 to 1.5 m.

Climbing, twining vine with masses
of dark-green, coarsely toothed
leaves. Tiny, round male flowers
appear in branched clusters, while
the larger female flowers hang in
cones beneath soft-green bracts.

*W*hen I was a little girl, people talked
about hops in whispers. Back then, everyone knew
that you only grew hops to make beer. But while we
were writing this book, John Butler showed me that the
new hops shoots—the first few centimetres of soft, tender
growth—make a wonderful treat. He brought some scram-
bled eggs with hops to the office, and they were a smash.
Those eggs convinced me that hops deserves to be included
among my top 25 herbs and edible flowers.

Try these!

Humulus lupulus (green hops, common hops) ✳
Fast-growing, vigorous vine; most common variety

Humulus lupulus aurea (golden hops) ✳ Slower-growing
than green hops

Planting

Start with young plants purchased from a garden centre.

How much ❋ At least two plants.

When ❋ Plant anytime during the growing season, up to two or three weeks before the average date of the first fall frost.

Where ❋ Full sun or part shade; needs sturdy support (a trellis, fence, or large tree). Thrives in almost any soil. Space plants 1 to 1.5 m apart—they'll fill in quickly.

Care and Nurture

Hops is very easy to grow! Water young plants well until established. Hops is drought-tolerant once it's established, but it won't grow as quickly in dry conditions. It dies to the ground in the winter and emerges quickly the following spring, so cut back after the first hard frost in the fall.

Hops grows as much as 5 m in a single season.

Harvesting

The shoots and male flowers are edible.

For best flavour ❋ Pick spring shoots: they're the sweetest. For summer harvesting, pick new shoots emerging from the soil.

Leaves ❋ Shoots and young leaves on tips can be picked at any time during the growing season.

Flowers ❋ Male flowers should be picked just after they open.

Preserving the Harvest

Hops shoots deteriorate quickly and must be used fresh. They can be stored for a few hours in a bowl of ice-water in the refrigerator.

Tips

❋ Hops is easy to grow and makes a good garden screen. Grow gold and green-leaf varieties of hops together for a terrific display, but remember that the green variety is much more aggressive than the golden.

❋ Hops plants can live up to 50 years! Its vigorous, lush growth makes hops a wonderful screen plant.

Hops and Eggs

Hops shoots pair beautifully with eggs and hops grows so vigorously that you can make these dishes regularly.
—John

Hops Scrambled Eggs

½ cup	125 mL	hops shoots, blanched, drained, and chopped
3	3	medium eggs
⅓ cup	85 mL	milk
salt and ground black pepper, to taste		
2 tsp.	10 mL	butter

Blanch hops shoots for 3 minutes in lightly salted boiling water. Drain in a colander and rinse under cold water. In a small bowl, beat together the eggs and milk; season with salt and pepper. Add the hops. Warm a skillet over medium heat; add the butter. Add the egg mixture and cook until done, stirring occasionally, about 3 to 4 minutes. Serve immediately.

Hops and Parmesan Omelette

½ cup	125 mL	fresh hops shoots, blanched, drained, and chopped
3	3	medium eggs
1 tbsp.	15 mL	grated Parmesan cheese
salt and ground black pepper, to taste		
2 tsp.	10 mL	oil

Blanch hops shoots for 3 minutes in lightly salted boiling water. Drain in a colander and rinse under cold water. Beat the eggs; add the cheese and seasoning. Add the hops to the egg-cheese mixture. Over medium–high heat in a skillet, heat the oil. Cook the omelette, stirring until the liquid congeals, about 2 to 3 minutes. **Variation**✳ Add small amounts of your favourite finely chopped herbs. Parsley, basil, oregano, chives, and thyme are all delicious additions.

This tangy relish makes an excellent topping for toasted baguette slices, mini-pita breads, and open-face sandwiches.
—John

Summer Hops Relish

1 cup	250 mL	diced hops shoots
1 cup	250 mL	hot water
4 tbsp.	60 mL	capers
1 cup	250 mL	finely diced celery
1 cup	250 mL	finely diced red onion
³⁄4 cup	185 mL	diced red pepper
4 tbsp.	60 mL	chopped sun dried tomatoes
2 tbsp.	30 mL	chopped fresh thyme
2 tbsp.	30 mL	olive oil
1 tbsp.	15 mL	lemon juice
fresh-ground pepper, to taste		

In a microwave-safe dish, combine the diced hops shoots and the hot water. On high setting, poach the hops for 4 minutes; drain and cool. In a separate bowl, mix the remaining ingredients and stir in the hops shoots. Season to taste. Keep refrigerated in a sealed container.

Yield ✳ 3 cups (750 mL).

Hint ✳ Use only the tender ends of hops shoots; pick the shoots when they're 6 to 8 inches (15 to 20 cm) long.

Blanch young hops leaves to remove the bitter taste, chop, and add to soup.

Boil hops shoots in water for a few minutes with a few drops of lemon juice. Season and toss in butter, simmer in fresh cream and butter, or serve with a brown sauce or gravy.

lavender
Lavandula angustifolia

Perennial; borderline hardy in most parts of Canada.
Height 30 to 90 cm; spread 30 to 45 cm.
Small shrub bears narrow, downy grey leaves and aromatic,
   dark-pink, purple, or violet flowers on tall spikes.

Lavender is my favourite fragrance. I always associate
it with spruce trees, ginger ale, turkey, creamed corn, and
other scents of Christmas. Lavender soaps and sachets
were prized gifts when I was growing up, and the strong,
elegant fragrance always made me think of far-away
foreign lands. ✳ *The most fragrant of all herbs, lavender*
has a scent reminiscent of camphor or rosemary. In the
spring and early summer, when the greenhouse is really
busy, staff members like to walk through the glasshouse
(where we sell the herbs) and run their hands through
the lavender plants for a quick pick-me-up.

Try these!

***Lavandula angustifolia* 'Munstead'** ✳ Hardiest of all varieties, will stand
   −30°C with snow cover; lavender flowers

***Lavandula angustifolia* 'Hidcote'** ✳ Tender variety with silvery-grey
   foliage and dark-purple flowers; 45 to 60 cm

***Lavandula* x *intermedia* (English lavender)** ✳ Tender variety with
   grey-green foliage and light-blue to violet flowers

Planting

Lavender is difficult to grow from seed, because the seed is slow and erratic, so start with young plants purchased from a garden centre.

How much✵ At least two plants.

When✵ Early spring; can withstand a light frost.

Where✵ Full sun. Demands dry, sandy, very well-drained soil. Space plants 30 to 45 cm apart.

Care and Nurture

Lavender requires some care to grow well. Although commercial plantings of lavender can last up to 30 years, most of us are best off replacing our lavender plants about every 3 years: they tend to get tough and woody. Prune lightly in the spring to shape and remove any winter-killed growth. Never cut into old wood: it sets the plant back. Never prune when frost is imminent: a tender perennial, lavender is easily damaged and needs protection from cold. Heavy foliage in the fall helps to trap the snow for insulation.

Harvesting

Harvest leaves and flowers as needed throughout the season. Lavender leaves and flowers are not only edible, but can also be used in a variety of handicrafts and products for the home.

For best flavour✵ Harvest leaves just before the last flowers on each stalk have opened fully.

Leaves✵ Cut sprigs where they attach to the main growing stem; use whole or strip the leaves from the top down. Discard tough stems.

Flowers✵ Clip individual flowers from stems. Remove all green or brown bits from the flowers before eating.

Preserving the Harvest

Use flowers fresh, dried, or frozen; freeze fresh flowers as soon as you harvest them. Use leaves fresh or dried.

Lavender makes a perfect cut-flower.

Tips

* Here are some other lavender varieties you may want to try.

The hardy **L. angustifolia 'Rosea'** has rose flowers and reaches 40 to 45 cm.

Another hardy variety, **L. angustifolia 'Jean Davis',** has pale-pink flowers and reaches 45 to 60 cm.

Fringed lavender (L. dentata), a tender variety, has dark-green foliage and dense spikes of lightly fragrant, purple-blue flowers tipped with purple bracts; it is scented like a sweet blend of rosemary and lavender.

Tender **spike lavender (L. latifolia)** has grey-green foliage and fragrant mauve-blue flowers in narrow, branching spikes.

French lavender (L. stoechas), another tender variety, has grey-green foliage and fragrant dark-purple flowers; its balsam-like scent suggests a blend of rosemary and lavender

* I like to plant lavender near low-growing evergreens, on the prevailing wind side: the evergreens catch the snow and help it drift to protect the lavender.

* Lavender grows fairly slowly, so it's best to buy well-established plants, at least two years old.

The essential oil from lavender has powerful antiseptic qualities that can kill many common bacteria, including typhoid, diphtheria, streptococcus and pneumococcus. Glove makers in Grasse, France who used lavender to scent leather showed a resistance to the plague. They encouraged others to carry lavender to ward off the disease.

Lavender's name comes from the Latin *lavare* (to wash). The ancient Greeks and Romans used lavender in their washing water to add a fresh, clean scent to their clothes, much as we use fabric softeners today.

Lavender Shortbread Cookies

2 cups	500 mL	unsalted butter
1 cup	250 mL	granulated sugar
½ tsp.	2.5 mL	salt
4 cups	1 L	all-purpose flour
1 tbsp.	15 mL	fresh lavender flowers, finely chopped
1 tsp.	5 mL	ground cinnamon
1 tsp.	5 mL	pure orange extract

With a mixer, blend the butter and sugar at medium-low speed for 8 to 10 minutes; scrape down the sides of the bowl occasionally. When the mixture is light and fluffy, add the flour on low speed and blend, until the ingredients are well mixed. Add the lavender blossoms (see note on flower preparation, page 24), orange extract, and cinnamon; mix for 30 seconds on low speed. Shape the dough into a ball and refrigerate for 2 hours. On a floured surface, roll out the dough ¼ to ½ inch (0.5 to 1 cm) thick and stamp out the cookies with a 2-inch (5-cm) cutter or cut them into squares or diamonds. Prick the tops with a fork to create an attractive pattern. Place cut-outs on a cookie sheet and bake at 300°F (150°C) for 25 to 30 minutes.

Hint✱ Alternate method for shaping dough: Refrigerate unshaped dough for 30 minutes. On a floured surface, shape the dough into a 2-inch (5-cm) round sausage (make two sausages if the roll gets too long). Wrap the sausage in plastic wrap and refrigerate for 1½ hours. When the dough is cold, cut the cookies into ¼-inch (0.5-cm) thick slices. Place slices on a cookie sheet and bake at 300°F (150°C) for 25 to 30 minutes.

You can also make rose-petal shortbread. Substitute 1½ tbsp (25 mL) finely chopped rose petals and 1 tsp (5 mL) rosewater for the lavender, and proceed as directed.
—John

lemongrass
Cymbopogon citratus

Tender perennial.
Height 70 cm to 1.5 m; spread to 1 m.
Clump-forming, grass-like plant with
  slender, long-bladed leaves.

*N*ative to India and Sri Lanka, lemongrass can be
one of the fussier herbs to grow, but its fans feel it is well
worth the challenge. Pat Yeakley, my friend from Califor-
nia, tells me, "If I ever move, my lemongrass will move with
me. I wouldn't be without it. I simply don't cook without
lemongrass." Lemongrass benefits from long northern days, but
it loves the heat of the sun. Give lemongrass a hot, dry spot in
your garden, and it will flourish. ❈ Any dish complemented by
lemon can be enhanced with the addition of lemongrass. In cooler
climates, the bulbs will be smaller but also more tender.

Try these!

***Cymbopogon citratus* (West Indian lemongrass)**❈ The most commonly
  found variety; clump-forming, grass-like, bulbous stems

***Cymbopogon flexuosus* (East Indian lemongrass)**❈ Less commonly
  found; flavour and habit similar to *C. citratus*

Planting

Start with young plants purchased from a garden centre; seed is not readily available.

How much✻ At least two plants.

When✻ After danger of frost has passed.

Where✻ Full sun. Prefers well-drained, sandy soil. Space plants 60 to 90 cm apart.

Care and Nurture

Lemongrass requires some care to grow well. It's a thirsty plant, so water daily during hot spells. Dry plants won't look wilted, but they need water just the same. Don't let lemongrass get waterlogged. Good drainage, whether lemongrass is grown indoors or out, is essential to prevent root-rot. Potted lemongrass will keep indoors over the winter in a brightly lit area. Propagate by dividing clumps.

Harvesting

Only the bulbous growth of lemongrass is eaten. Cut the stem at the base of plant; discard any roots. Keep only the enlarged base and first 6 to 10 cm of the lower stalk. Discard the leaves and tough outer stalk.

For best flavour✻ Harvest lemongrass late in the season, when the bulbous bases are large and fleshy.

Leaves✻ Not eaten.

Flowers✻ Not eaten.

Preserving the Harvest

Lemongrass is best eaten fresh or preserved by freezing: dried lemongrass gets tough and fibrous. Wrap the peeled, whole base and lower stalk in plastic wrap and freeze in a plastic bag. Wrap well to prevent the strong flavour from infiltrating other foods.

Plant lemongrass in full sun in a warm location.

Tips

✻ The outer sheaths of lemongrass are very tough. Peel the stalk to expose the more tender layers; pulverize it to release the flavour. Toss the tough remains on the barbecue coals to produce lemon-scented smoke.

✻ Use the dried leaf-blades in potpourris and sachets.

Shrimp and Lemongrass
Hot and Sour Soup

*Fresh lemongrass, sealed in plastic,
is available at Asian food markets.
Frozen, it will last 4 to
5 months—right through
the cold months!*
—John

3 10-oz. cans	3 284-mL cans	chicken bouillon
or		
4 cups	1 L	chicken stock
2	2	kaffir lime leaves, finely chopped
1 tbsp.	15 mL	finely chopped lemongrass
3 tbsp.	45 mL	lime juice
3 tbsp.	45 mL	fish sauce
2 tsp.	10 mL	hot chili sauce
½ tsp.	2.5 mL	sugar
10	10	drained and sliced straw mushrooms
12	12	raw shrimp, peeled and deveined
2	2	chopped green onions

In a medium saucepan over medium heat,
warm the stock. Add the lime leaves,
lemongrass, lime juice, fish sauce, chili sauce,
and sugar. Bring to a boil and simmer for
3 minutes. Add the mushrooms and shrimp;
cook for 2 to 3 minutes. Ladle soup into
bowls and garnish with green onions.

Note ❋ Kaffir lime leaves are available fresh
or dried at Asian food markets. I keep the
fresh ones in the freezer and the dried ones
in a sealed container. Fish sauce is available
at Asian/Vietnamese food markets. It is made
from fermented anchovies and is quite salty,
with a very pungent aroma. Straw mushrooms
are found at Asian food markets, sometimes
fresh but usually canned.

Variation ❋ Add cooked crab or lobster meat
(fresh, frozen, or canned) with the mushrooms
and shrimp. Or add 4 oz. (100 g) thinly sliced
pork, beef, or chicken before the mushrooms
and shrimp. Cook for 2 to 3 minutes, then
continue with recipe as directed.

95

For a stronger flavour, garnish this dish
with finely chopped lemon balm.
—John

Rice with Lemongrass, Green Onions, and Chives

2 tbsp.	30 mL	vegetable oil
1	1	medium onion, finely chopped
¼ tsp.	1 mL	turmeric
1½ cups	375 mL	long-grain rice
2 cups	500 mL	chicken stock, broth, **or** bouillon
2 stalks	2 stalks	lemongrass, cut into 3-inch lengths
3	3	green onions, chopped
1 tbsp.	15 mL	chives, chopped
salt and white pepper		
chopped cilantro for garnish		

In a medium saucepan over medium heat, warm half the oil. Add the onion and turn the heat down to medium-low. Add the turmeric and sauté 5 minutes, stirring occasionally. Stir in the rice and mix well to coat grains. Add the chicken stock and lemongrass. Increase heat to medium and bring liquid to a simmer. Reduce heat to medium-low, cover pot with lid, and cook for 15 to 18 minutes, or until the rice is tender. Remove from the heat and let the rice stand, covered, for 7 to 8 minutes. Remove and discard lemongrass pieces. In a large pan, warm the remaining oil at medium heat. Add the green onions and chives; heat for 1 minute. Add the cooked rice and sauté until heated through, about 3 to 4 minutes. Season to taste. Serve with chopped cilantro for garnish.

Lemon peel can substitute for lemongrass in recipes. When substituting, add a small amount of galangal powder or freshly grated ginger with the peel.

*Use the trimmings from the
lemongrass stems on the barbecue
grill to add flavoured smoke while
the fish is cooking.*
—John

Trout with Lemongrass

4 6-oz.	4 180-g	trout
12 stalks	12 stalks	lemongrass, trimmed to 6-inch (15-cm) lengths
salt and ground black pepper, to taste		
¼ cup	65 mL	melted butter, clarified
¼ cup	65 mL	vegetable oil
1 tbsp.	15 mL	fresh lime **or** lemon juice
2	2	lemons, cut into wedges

Dry the fish with paper towel and place
3 stems of lemongrass in the cavity of each
fish. Using a very sharp knife, score the side
of the fish through the skin. The cuts should
be diagonal and not too deep. Make 3 cuts
on each side. Add salt and pepper to taste.
Pour the melted butter and oil onto a
baking sheet or shallow ovenproof dish big
enough to hold the fish. Place the sheet or
dish on the barbecue at medium heat; allow
the oil and butter to heat for 5 minutes.
Put fish on sheet and cook 5 to 7 minutes.
Carefully turn the fish over and cook until
the fish flakes easily, about 5 to 7 minutes.
Squeeze fresh lime or lemon juice over the
fish just before serving. Serve with lemon
wedges and Herb Butter (see page 30).

A versatile herb in the kitchen, lemongrass is a
welcome addition to curries, soups, rice stews,
sauces, chicken and seafood dishes, and marinades.

marigolds

Calendula officinalis, Tagetes spp.

Annuals; may self-sow.

Pot marigold (*Calendula officinalis*): Height 20 to 50 cm; spread 20 to 30 cm. Flowers closely resemble chrysanthemums.

African marigold (*Tagetes erecta*): Height 15 to 90 cm; spread 30 to 45 cm. Tall plants with large, round, solidly coloured flowers.

French marigold (*Tagetes patula*): Height 15 to 30 cm; spread 15 to 20 cm. Shorter plants; flowers vary in colour, size, and petal type.

Signet marigold (*Tagetes signata*): Height to 30 cm; spread 30 to 45 cm. Fragrant plants with lacy, fern-like foliage and masses of tiny, brightly coloured single flowers; mounding growth habit.

Years ago, one of my friends made some marigold muffins. I was keen to try them, knowing she was a health-conscious gardener. But it took all my self-control to finish the muffin after taking the first bite. They were terrible! It was only later that I learned she had made them with French marigolds.

❁ All marigolds are edible, but pot and signet marigolds taste best. African and French marigolds make gorgeous garnishes, but don't bother eating them.

Try these!

***Calendula officinalis* (pot marigold, English marigold)** ❁ Mildly spicy flavour; available in a wide range of colours

***Tagetes signata* (signet marigold, rock garden marigold)** ❁ Flavour is best of all marigolds, like a spicy tarragon

Tagetes marigolds have a uniform, mounding growth habit.

Planting

Marigolds and calendula are best grown from young plants purchased from a garden centre. However, both can be started indoors from seed or seeded directly into the garden as soon as the ground is workable.

How much✻ At least six plants; more for ornamental use.

When✻ About one week after the date of average last spring frost.

Where✻ Full sun; will tolerate some light shade. Good in containers and borders. Prefers rich, well-drained soil. Space plants 15 to 45 cm apart.

Care and Nurture

Marigolds are easy to grow! Deadhead regularly to encourage continuous blooming.

orange tagetes

Calendulas are native to the Canary Islands and south-central Europe and Asia. In ancient Rome, peasants couldn't afford saffron, so they used powdered calendula petals as a substitute. Early Indian and Arabic cultures used calendulas to colour fabrics, foods, and cosmetics.

French marigolds have a strong, often bitter, flavour but make attractive garnishes.

Harvesting

Cut flowers often: the more you cut, the more these plants will bloom. Young calendula leaves can be served boiled or steamed as a green vegetable.

For best flavour✳ Harvest mid-morning, after the dew has evaporated and before the day gets too hot.

Leaves✳ Pick smaller, more tender leaves for mildest flavour. Cut leaf stalk and use whole.

Flowers✳ Harvest as soon as the flowers open. Clip flower head from stalk; pick off the outer petals and discard the bitter centre.

Preserving the Harvest

Use flowers fresh, or dry petals immediately for best flavour. To dry, spread petals on screens and put them in a warm, dark, dust-free area with good ventilation. Store dried petals in an airtight jar. Use leaves immediately: they do not store well.

The pungent lemony
fragrance of tagetes foliage
is reputed to repel insects.
Brushing the leaves as you
walk by releases their
fresh, clean scent.

Tips

* Use French and African marigolds for colourful garnishes and attractive table settings, but don't bother eating them in large quantities, because their flavour is strong and bitter. They're the least palatable marigolds, although they are safely edible.

* Pot marigolds can stall (stop blooming due to high temperatures) in the midsummer heat. Make sure to water well when the weather is hot. I plant my calendulas in areas that get light shade in the late afternoon and they usually bloom throughout the summer.

* Signet marigolds make an excellent choice for windy locations such as balconies. Both signet marigolds and calendulas are excellent for container growing.

Pot marigolds were said to bloom on the calends (first day of the month)—hence the Latin name *Calendula*.

According to the Victorian language of flowers, signet marigolds signify jealousy.

Warm, moist, and delicious comfort food—serve with a flavourful coffee prepared from freshly ground beans!
—Joyce

Coffeecake with Marmalade and Marigolds

½ cup	125 mL	soft butter
1 cup	250 mL	sugar
2	2	large eggs
2 cups	500 mL	flour
1 tsp.	5 mL	baking powder
1 tsp.	5 mL	baking soda
½ tsp.	2 mL	salt
1 cup	250 mL	buttermilk
1 tsp.	5 mL	vanilla
½ cup	125 mL	Seville orange marmalade
⅓ cup	75 mL	marigold petals
natural **or** orange yogourt		
marigold flowers		
Topping		
⅓ cup	75 mL	brown sugar
¼ cup	50 mL	sugar
1 tsp.	5 mL	cinnamon
½ cup	125 mL	chopped nuts **or** coarsely broken saltines

With a hand mixer, beat together butter, sugar, eggs, flour, baking powder, baking soda, salt, buttermilk, and vanilla until smooth and fluffy. Spoon half the batter into a well-greased 13 x 9-inch (33 x 23-cm) baking pan. Drop the marmalade by small spoonfuls over the batter. Blend carefully together. Sprinkle batter with marigold petals (see note on flower preparation, page 24); top with remaining batter. Spread batter evenly with the back of an oiled spatula. Swirl a knife gently through the batter to create a rippled effect. Combine topping ingredients and sprinkle evenly over batter. Bake at 350°F (180°C) for 30 minutes. Serve each warm piece topped with a spoonful of yogourt and a marigold.

Note❋ Saltines make an economical and safe substitute for nuts. Do not cover the cake or they will lose their crunchy texture!

Try this dish with rose or violet petals in place of the marigolds.
—John

Sweet Couscous

1 cup	250 g	quick-cooking couscous
¼ cup	60 mL	yellow raisins
2 tbsp.	30 mL	butter
4 tbsp.	60 mL	sugar
2 to 4 drops	2 to 4 drops	rosewater
1 tbsp.	15 mL	marigold petals
salt, to taste		
1 cup	250 mL	whipping cream (optional)

In a large saucepan, cook the couscous as directed on the package. Soak the raisins in warm water for 10 minutes. Add the butter to the couscous and fluff with a fork. Drain the raisins and add to couscous. Stir in the sugar, rosewater, and marigold petals (see note on flower preparation, page 24); add salt to taste. Serve hot, with whipping cream on the side, if desired.

To make calendula dye, chop petals very finely or pulverize them with a mortar and pestle. The beautiful coloured paste can be added to rice, butter, or any food that would benefit from a rich golden colour.

Powdered calendula is often used as a substitute for saffron in rice.

A wonderful ending to a summer dinner party, especially after fresh trout, salmon, or chicken.
—Joyce

❧

Signet marigolds taste something like a spicy tarragon and possess a pleasant lemon scent. The white part of the petal, near the base, should be removed because it has a bitter flavour.

Chilled Orange Soufflé with Calendula

4	4	large eggs, separated
1 cup	250 mL	sugar, divided
¼ cup	50 mL	frozen concentrated orange juice, thawed
¼ cup	50 mL	lemon juice
grated peel of 1 lemon		
grated peel of 1 orange		
dash	dash	salt
1 tbsp.	15 mL	unflavoured gelatin
¼ cup	50 mL	orange liqueur
1 cup	250 mL	whipping cream
yellow and orange food colouring		
¼ cup	50 mL	yellow and orange calendula petals
fresh orange slices		
yellow and orange calendula flowers		

Beat egg yolks until light and fluffy. Add ½ cup (125 mL) sugar gradually; beat until very light in colour. Blend in juices, peel, and a dash of salt. Stir over low heat until slightly thickened. Soak gelatin in liqueur and stir into hot custard. Cool. Colour a lovely orange tone with approximately 2 drops orange and 1 drop yellow food colouring. (Remember colour will lighten with egg whites and cream!) Beat egg whites until foamy, adding remaining ½ cup (125 mL) sugar gradually. Beat until stiff. Whip cream. Fold egg whites into custard with a whisk and then gently fold in whipped cream and calendula petals (see note on flower preparation, page 24). Pour into a beautiful crystal bowl or glass soufflé dish. Chill. (May also be frozen, but texture of petals will naturally change.) To serve, top with paper-thin orange slices and calendula flowers. Serves 6.

mint

Mentha spp.

Hardy perennial.
Height 15 to 60 cm; spread indefinite.
Vigorous, aggressive plant with dark-
  green leaves on erect, square stems.

*You don't require much of a green
thumb to grow mint successfully. Mint is a
vigorous, invasive plant, so I like to keep it in
containers. But it's so aggressive that it will even escape its container!
A couple of years ago, I put my potted mint on the back patio.
Before I knew it, shoots had grown over the edge of the pot and
into the patio blocks. The following year, I had mint growing
right from the patio!* ❋ *Mint comes in a huge variety of enticing
scents and flavours. Start with a standard like spearmint, try a
fruity variety like grapefruit or pineapple mint, then let your
senses be your guide.*

Try these!

***Mentha spicata* (spearmint, English mint)** ❋ Best cooking mint
  —my favourite!

***Mentha* x *piperita piperita* (peppermint, candy mint)** ❋ Wonderful
  peppermint flavour

***Mentha suaveolens* (apple mint, round-leaf mint)** ❋ Minty apple-
  menthol fragrance

Planting

Start with young plants purchased from a garden centre, or split a clump from an established plant.

How much✳ One plant of each type you enjoy.

When✳ As soon as the soil is warm enough to work.

Where✳ Full sun; will tolerate light shade. Invasive—should be grown in containers. Prefers rich, moist soil; will grow almost anywhere. Plants are invasive; keep separated by 60 to 90 cm.

One kilogram of mint oil can flavour 100,000 sticks of gum.

Care and Nurture

Mint is easy to grow! Keep the soil moist: mint requires lots of water. In cold regions, mint needs heavy snow cover to survive the winter. Mint needs to be renewed every 3 to 4 years, because the centre gets old, tough, and woody and eventually dies out. Renew mint by thinning the bed, dividing the plant, and giving some away to friends and neighbours. Mint should be replaced with another crop every 4 to 5 years: solid stands of mint—known as "meadow mint"—are vulnerable to rust disease. Remember that any mint roots you leave in the ground will grow into new plants.

Harvesting

Mint grows so vigorously that you can often harvest the whole plant twice in a growing season. Gather stems together in one hand and cut them about 10 cm from the ground.

Mint is extremely vigorous, so plant it in a large container.

spearmint

pineapple mint

For best flavour❋ Harvest just as flowering begins.

Leaves❋ Harvest individual leaves by clipping the leaf stalk where it attaches to the plant stem. Cut sprigs and use whole, or strip the leaves. Discard tough stalks.

Flowers❋ Pick as they appear. Clip the flower stalk where it attaches to the plant stem; discard stalk.

Preserving the Harvest

Mint is best used fresh, but it is easily dried, frozen, or preserved in oil or vinegar. Store fresh mint, stems down, in a glass of water covered with a plastic bag; refrigerate. Change the water every 2 days, and it will keep for a week. Mint flowers should be used the same day they are picked. They will keep in the fridge for a short time, but their flavour fades quickly. Mint flowers can be preserved in oil, butter, or vinegar, but they do not freeze well. Mint leaves can also be crystallized (see pages 134–35).

In Greek mythology, Hades, Lord of the Underworld, wooed the beautiful nymph Minthe, which made Hades' wife, Sephony, extremely jealous. Furious, Sephony turned Minthe into a plant—the plant that we call mint.

peppermint

Tips

* While peppermint and spearmint are the most important culinary mints, there are plenty of others; indeed, there are more than 30 species and 600 varieties of mint! The best way to select a plant is by nose rather than by name, but here are some varieties you might want to try.
Curled spearmint
(**M. spicata 'Crispa'**) has mild spearmint flavour.
Pineapple mint (M. suaveolens 'variegata') is similar to apple mint, but its flavour is fruitier and sweeter.
Ginger mint (M. x gracilis 'variegata', aka Metha x gentillis) has a fruity fragrance with a hint of ginger.

* Don't buy mint seeds! Mint varieties grown from commercially available seed strains are greatly inferior to the cultivated varieties propagated by cuttings or division.

* If you grow mint in containers in a cool region, you must sink the pots into the ground in the fall to enable the mint to survive the winter. The ground acts as insulation to protect the plant. When spring returns, dig up the pot and pull out the root ball. Cut off the bottom one-third to one-half of the roots, and remove any old, woody core. Replant the root clump with new potting mix.

Corsican mint is a great choice for rock gardens, contributing a fresh, clean scent and an inconspicuous beauty. It is less aggressive than other mints and forms a low-growing carpet. It also attracts bees and butterflies.

apple mint

variegated mint

Minted Chicken Soup

When homemade soups are refrigerated for a day or two, some of the flavours infuse, blending and becoming more subtle. This soup tastes even better the second day!
—John

3 10-oz. cans	3 284-mL cans	chicken bouillon
or		
4 cups	1 L	chicken stock
3	3	boneless, skinless chicken breasts
1	1	bay leaf
1 sprig		thyme
4 sprigs		parsley
¾ cup	175 mL	cooked long-grain rice
1 tbsp.	15 mL	lemon **or** lime juice
6 tbsp.	90 mL	chopped fresh mint
salt and ground black pepper, to taste		
1	1	lemon, thinly sliced

In a medium saucepan over medium heat, warm the chicken bouillon or stock; add the chicken breasts. Bring to a boil and lower heat to a simmer; skim the stock to remove any impurities. Add the bay leaf, thyme, and parsley. Simmer for 30 minutes, again skimming off any impurities. Remove the chicken meat and cool. Remove the bay leaf, thyme, and parsley stems. Add the cooked rice and simmer for 2 minutes. Cut the chicken into clean dice. Add diced chicken to soup with the lime or lemon juice. Add the chopped mint and seasoning. Serve soup over sprigs of fresh mint. Garnish with lemon slices.

Note ✳ Dried mint may be substituted for fresh—use 1 to 2 tbsp. (15 to 30 mL). The flavour will be changed very subtly.

Hint ✳ This soup may be refrigerated for 2 to 3 days. It also freezes well.

*Serve this quick sauce with
Samosas (page 56).*
—John

Fresh Mint Chutney

2 cups	500 mL	fresh mint leaves, firmly packed
1	1	medium onion, diced
½ cup	125 mL	chopped fresh parsley
⅓ cup	85 mL	lemon juice
4 tbsp.	60 mL	sugar
2 tsp.	10 mL	salt
½ tsp.	2.5 mL	cayenne pepper

In a blender, grind the mint, onion, parsley, lemon juice, sugar, salt, and cayenne pepper. Blend until the mixture forms a paste; scrape the sides of the blender to ensure even blending. Serve with lamb. Will keep in the refrigerator for 2 to 3 days.

Mint sauce served with lamb aids the digestion—it makes the fibres of the young meat more digestible.

Fold sliced strawberries or raspberries and slivered mint into slightly softened vanilla ice cream. Re-freeze and serve with chocolate sugar cookies.

Tender, juicy, and oh so delicious!
—Joyce

Lamb with Sherry, Mint, and Garlic

6	6	lamb steaks
or		
12	12	tiny loin chops
2 tbsp.	25 mL	chopped fresh mint
1 tbsp.	15 mL	black peppercorns
1	1	onion, chopped
2	2	garlic cloves, crushed
¼ cup	50 mL	oil
½ cup	125 mL	dry (definitely not sweet) sherry
1 tsp.	5 mL	Worcestershire sauce

Add finely chopped mint to your favourite rhubarb jam recipe.

Lightly slash edges of steaks or chops. Process the mint, peppercorns, onion, and garlic until puréed. Add remaining ingredients and process lightly to combine. Coat steaks with the mixture, place in a plastic-covered shallow dish, and refrigerate 8 hours or overnight. Barbecue or broil the lamb on high heat until crusty on the outside but still pink and juicy on the inside, approximately 3 minutes on each side. Baste meat with marinade as it cooks. Serves 6. Serve with fresh corn brushed with herb butter and a stir-fry of all those wonderful summer vegetables (baby carrots, sugar peas, tiny zucchini, Bright Lights Swiss chard, Sweet Million tomatoes, cucumber chunks, radishes), any herbs, and a bit of sorrel. **Note** ❋ May also be made with a boned leg of lamb.

A light yet satisfying dessert!
—John

Minted Meringues

3	3	egg whites
pinch	pinch	salt
¼ tsp.	1 mL	cream of tartar
1 cup	250 mL	sugar
2 tsp.	10 mL	cocoa powder
1 tsp.	5 mL	pure vanilla essence
½ tsp.	2.5 mL	peppermint extract
2 pinches	2 pinches	dried mint leaves

With an electric mixer in a large bowl, beat the egg whites with the salt until they are foamy. Add cream of tartar and continue to beat the whites until they hold soft peaks; set aside. In a small bowl, mix the cocoa powder and sugar. Add the cocoa-sugar mixture to the egg whites a spoonful at a time, beating well after each addition. Continue to beat until the meringues hold stiff peaks. With a rubber spatula, fold in the vanilla, peppermint extract, and dried mint leaves. Drop spoonfuls of the meringue mixture 2 to 3 inches (5 to 8 cm) apart on a baking sheet lined with parchment. Bake the meringues in preheated oven at 200°F (100°C) for 1 hour and 15 minutes. The meringues should be light and dry. Remove the meringues and cool on a rack. Store in sealed containers on layers of paper towel.

nasturtiums

Tropaeolum majus

Annual.

Height 20 to 30 cm; spread 20 to 30 cm.
Trailing types may reach 60 cm.

Plants have mounding dark-green foliage and medium-sized, slightly fragrant, semi-double and double flowers with crinkled petals. Vegetative and seed-propagated varieties have distinct growth habits.

I *don't recall when I first learned that nasturtiums were edible, but I do remember my mother's reaction when I told her that people eat them. She calmly watered her plants and scoffed, "No, they don't." I could tell she'd never heard anything so stupid. Years later, I suggested we add nasturtiums to a salad Mom had made. She consented, but she didn't like them at all. I think they were too hot for her liking.* ❋ *I, on the other hand, love nasturtiums: they taste as good as they look! The spicy, peppery flowers and leaves can be used in a range of dishes, and the colourful plants are among the prettiest annuals I grow.*

Try these!

Whirlybird series ❋ Seed-propagated nasturtiums with gorgeous single flowers—very showy; bushy growth habit; blooms more profusely than other seed varieties and produces blossoms on top of the foliage rather than under the leaves

Apricot Twist ❋ Vegetatively propagated; double apricot-orange blooms

Hermine Grashoff ❋ Vegetatively propagated; bright-reddish orange double flowers

Forest Flame ❋ My favourite vegetative variety, with bright apricot-orange, red-splashed double flowers and cream-and-green variegated leaves; looks gorgeous in salads

Planting

When growing nasturtiums, the most important thing to note is that seed-propagated varieties and vegetatively propagated varieties have very different care requirements. Seed varieties require less care, but with a bit more work, vegetative varieties offer massive numbers of blooms. If you want to grow the more-robust vegetative nasturtiums, you'll need to buy young plants from a garden centre, because these varieties do not produce viable seed.

How much✳ Two or three plants; more for ornamental use.

When✳ One week after the date of average last spring frost.

Where✳ Full sun to light shade. Excellent in containers or hanging baskets. Vegetative nasturtiums like rich soil; seed varieties prefer average or poor soil. Space each plant 20 to 30 cm apart in the garden, 15 cm apart in pots.

Care and Nurture

Nasturtiums are easy to grow! Water thoroughly, but only when soil is dry. Vegetative nasturtiums require heavy feeding, but seed nasturtiums require little, if any, fertilizer. Vegetative nasturtiums should be pinched and deadheaded regularly to promote continuous flowering and bushy growth.

All parts of the nasturtium are edible.

Harvesting

All parts of the nasturtium are edible—the leaves, the flower buds, and the flowers. The buds can be used as a substitute for capers or like a mild peppercorn in salads.

Traditional nasturtium varieties attract humming-birds and bees. But the spurs cause the flowers to face the ground, hiding them under the foliage. We recommend spurless varieties such as the Whirlybird series, so that the flowers are held well above the foliage, creating a much more colourful display. Nasturtium spurs contain a sweet nectar and are considered a delicacy.

For best flavour✻ Choose young, tender growth—young leaves and newly opened flowers.

Leaves✻ Clip the leaf stalk where it attaches to the main growing stem; cut stalk off leaf body and discard.

Flower buds✻ Harvest while the bud is still tightly closed. Clip cleanly from the stalk.

Flowers✻ Harvest flowers after they have opened fully. Clip the stalk two or three centimetres from the base of flower head.

single flower of the 'Whirlybird' nasturtium

double flower of the 'Apricot Twist' nasturtium

Preserving the Harvest

Leaves, flowers, and buds should be used fresh. They cannot be dried or frozen, but may be refrigerated briefly.

The name nasturtium is derived from the Latin words *nasus tortus* (twisted or convulsed nose), a reference to the plant's pungent scent.

Tips

* If the plants get leggy, don't be afraid to cut them back. I cut my plants back quite severely, then water and fertilize well. They grow back with a vengeance, although they look ugly for a few days. If you're planning a week or two of holidays, cut the plants back by up to a third before you leave. By the time you return, the plants will have reflushed.

* Nasturtiums are a good choice for children's gardens because the pea-sized seeds are big enough to be easily handled by small fingers and the plants grow very quickly, with big, bright flowers.

* Nasturtiums come in a variety of colours, including cherry, gold, mahogany, orange, peach, and scarlet, with new shades making their debut each year.

Make nasturtium vinegar by pickling the blossoms. Pick young flower buds, wash them, and pickle them in salted vinegar in bottles with shallots, garlic, and red pepper for about a month.

Instead of using just lettuce, add tiny beet leaves, radish leaves, Swiss chard leaves, and any herb that appeals.
—Joyce

Nasturtium Salad with Bacon and Croutons

8 cups	2 L	salad greens
¼ cup	50 mL	chopped cilantro
¼ cup	50 mL	small nasturtium leaves
¼ cup	50 mL	chopped chives
10 slices	10 slices	bacon, cooked crisp and crumbled
⅓ cup	75 mL	toasted walnuts **or** pecans
½ cup	125 mL	herb croutons, homemade **or** purchased
nasturtium flowers		

Combine all ingredients in a salad bowl and toss with a small amount of mustard dressing. Serve immediately, garnished with nasturtium flowers (see note on flower preparation, page 24).

Mustard Dressing

3 tbsp.	50 mL	white-wine **or** rice-wine vinegar
2 tbsp.	25 mL	extra-virgin olive oil
1 tsp.	5 mL	aged balsamic vinegar
2 tsp.	10 mL	liquid honey
2 tsp.	10 mL	Dijon mustard
1	1	clove garlic, crushed
freshly ground black pepper		

Whisk ingredients together thoroughly.

Serve fritters with Fresh Fruit Salad (see pages 194–95).
—John

Sweet Fritters

1⅓ cups	330 mL	all-purpose flour
3 tbsp.	45 mL	granulated sugar
2	2	medium eggs
2 tbsp.	30 mL	soft butter
1 tbsp.	15 mL	light rum
1 tsp.	5 mL	grated lemon **or** orange peel
1 tbsp.	15 mL	nasturtium petals
pinch	pinch	salt
pinch	pinch	cinnamon (optional)

oil for deep-frying
icing sugar, to finish

Sift the flour into a large bowl and make a well in the centre. Add the eggs, butter, sugar, rum, grated rind, nasturtium petals (see note on flower preparation, page 24), salt, and cinnamon (if desired). Blend the mixture by hand until it forms a soft dough. Do not overmix. If the dough is too sticky, add 1 to 2 tbsp. (15 to 30 mL) of flour and mix in gently. Form the dough into a ball and cover with plastic wrap. Refrigerate at least two hours. Divide the dough into quarters. Work with one quarter and refrigerate the rest. On a floured surface, roll the dough out paper thin. Cut the dough into 3-inch (8-cm) rectangles. Heat the oil to 350°F (180°C). Fry fritters in oil, turning with metal tongs with they are golden-brown. Drain fritters on paper towels, then sprinkle with icing sugar. Repeat with remaining dough. Serve immediately. **Yield** ✳ 24 fritters.

oregano & marjoram

Origanum spp.

Perennials; normally grown as annuals in colder climates
(except sweet marjoram, which is an annual in all climates).
Height 20 to 40 cm; spread 20 to 40 cm.
Lush green herbs with clusters of very small, tubular, mauve,
pink or white flowers; grow as a groundcover.

*O*regano and marjoram are popular herbs, but they cause
some confusion among gardeners. They're so closely related
that they can be virtually indistinguishable. And adding to
the problem is the fact that oregano is the Spanish name for
marjoram. If you are buying oregano and marjoram,
it pays to ask for them by their Latin names to ensure
you get what you want. ❋ The best oregano for
cooking is Greek oregano; the best marjoram, sweet
marjoram. I use Greek oregano often: it's bright and punchy!
I like to call it the "pizza herb," but its flavour is really versatile.
I use sweet marjoram for a sweeter, subtler taste.

Try these!

Origanum majorana (**sweet marjoram**) ❋ Annual; strong spicy flavour

Origanum majorana aureum (**golden marjoram**) ❋ Annual; similar to
sweet marjoram but milder in flavour

Origanum vulgare hirtum (**Greek oregano, true oregano**) ❋ Hardy
perennial; strong, excellent flavour—my favourite!

Origanum vulgare hirtum var. **'Kaliteri'** ❋ High oil content and wonderful flavour (the variety name means "best" in Greek)

Planting

Oregano must be started from young plants purchased from a garden centre. Marjoram may be started indoors from seed or grown from young plants purchased from a garden centre.

How much ❋ Two or three plants.

When ❋ About one week after the date of the average last spring frost.

Marjoram and oregano leaves can be rubbed over heavy oak furniture and floors to impart a fresh, fragrant polish.

Where ❋ Full sun; sheltered. Golden varieties need a bit of shade in the afternoon to prevent the leaves from scorching. Excellent in containers. Prefers well-drained soil. Space plants 20 to 60 cm apart.

Care and Nurture

Origanum species are easy to grow! Pinch back to encourage branching and bushy growth. To prevent root-rot, never overwater plants.

Oregano is an excellent container plant.

Greek oregano

Italian oregano

Harvesting

You can harvest the leaves or the flowers. The flowers have a strong flavour, so use them sparingly. Be sure to pull each flower from its socket (calyx)—you don't want any of the green bits.

For best flavour❋ Harvest leaves after the flower buds have formed but before they have opened.

Leaves❋ Harvest as needed throughout the growing season. Cut sprigs 6 to 10 cm from the ground. Use whole or strip the leaves; discard tough stems or use on the barbecue for flavouring.

Flowers❋ Harvest flowers shortly after they open. Flowers grow in clusters; clip cluster from growing stem and pull gently into individual florets.

Preserving the Harvest

Oregano and marjoram dry well—in fact, unlike many herbs, their flavours actually become more intense after drying. These herbs are also suitable for freezing.

golden oregano

purple oregano

oregano flowers

It was once believed that sweet marjoram could keep milk from spoiling, hence the adjective "sweet."

Tips

* Wild or common oregano (*Origanum vulgare*) is a poor variety, with a bland flavour and aroma. It is, however, available as seed at garden centres. I don't recommend that you grow this variety, when there are so many better plants to choose from.

* Growers have recently developed ornamental *Origanum* varieties. These plants are gorgeous, with loads of flowers and a compact, mounding growth-habit; they bloom right through the season, and the flowers attract butterflies and bees. Just don't try to eat them!

* In areas where winters are more severe, protect perennial species by mulching or building up a heavy snow cover.

Marjoram and oregano look great in rock gardens. Golden oregano makes a good contrast plant for herb gardens.

If the ancient Greeks spotted oregano growing on a grave, it meant that the departed was happy in the afterlife.

sweet marjoram

*This recipe requires some effort,
but the flavour is worth it!*
—John

Stuffed Vine Leaves

2 tbsp.	30 mL	olive oil
1	1	medium onion, finely diced
1 lb.	450 g	lean ground beef
2 tbsp.	30 mL	fresh oregano, chopped
or		
1 tbsp.	15 mL	dried oregano
salt and black pepper, to taste		
3 cups	750 mL	cooked long-grain rice
18	18	large vine leaves
1 cup	250 mL	chicken broth **or** stock
1	1	lemon cut into wedges

In a skillet over medium heat, warm the olive oil. Add the diced onions and sauté for 5 minutes, stirring constantly. Add the ground beef, breaking into fine pieces using a wooden spoon or spatula. Stir constantly until the meat is fully cooked, about 6 to 7 minutes. Drain any excess oil. Add the oregano, lemon juice, and salt and pepper to taste. In a large bowl, mix the cooked rice and the flavoured meat. Cool the mixture. Rinse the vine leaves under cold running water. Trim off the stems. Lay out the leaves with the tips facing away from you. Place a portion of filling in each leaf. Fold over the outside edges of the leaves to encase the filling. Fold the leaf towards the tip, turning

Add finely chopped fresh marjoram
to cheese scones or biscuits.

the side points in. Repeat until all the leaves are filled. Place the stuffed, rolled leaves, seam side down, in a casserole dish. Heat chicken stock. Pour over the vine leaves. Cover with a lid or put a dish directly on top of the leaves to weight them down slightly. Bake the vine leaves at 325°F (160°C) for 25 to 30 minutes. Serve hot or cold with lemon slices or wedges.

Variations ❋ Add ¼ cup (60 mL) pitted, sliced black olives to the recipe along with the cooked rice. Or follow the same method but replace the ground beef and oregano with red snapper and dill **or** with lean ground lamb and mint, both in the same proportions. (Add 1 tsp. [5 mL] of lemon juice with the lamb.)

Note ❋ Vine leaves come packed in brine in jars; they can be found at Middle Eastern or Greek grocery stores and in the ethnic food section of most major grocery stores.

Oregano is added to commercial chili powders, chili beans, and other strongly flavoured dishes containing chilis, garlic, and onions —it complements such flavours well.

Pasta with Summer Herbs and Tomatoes

Cooked baby shrimp make a great addition! Serve with a mixed green salad and rye bread.
—Joyce

2 cups	500 mL	spiral pasta
extra-virgin olive oil		
1 or 2	1 or 2	garlic cloves, crushed
2 tbsp.	25 mL	extra-virgin olive oil
2	2	large, very ripe tomatoes, peeled, seeded, and diced
1 tbsp.	15 mL	chopped fresh oregano
2 tbsp.	25 mL	chopped fresh basil
1 tbsp.	15 mL	chopped fresh thyme
2 tbsp.	25 mL	chopped fresh parsley
2 tbsp.	25 mL	freshly squeezed lemon juice
1 tsp.	5 mL	finely grated lemon peel
salt and pepper, to taste		
freshly grated Parmesan cheese		

Chop oregano or marjoram leaves finely and add to butter or butter sauces for fish.

Cook pasta in lots of water just until *al dente*. Drain and toss with a small amount of oil. Keep warm in a covered casserole. Sauté garlic in 2 tbsp. (25 mL) of oil. Add all remaining ingredients, except Parmesan, and cook only until tomatoes are hot. Toss thoroughly with pasta and serve immediately. Offer pepper and Parmesan cheese at the table. Serves 3 to 4.

*Similar to French toast,
but savoury. Try it for
brunch or supper.*
—John

Herb and
Cheese Toast

Marjoram leaves can be infused
and served as an aromatic tea.

4	4	eggs
½ cup	125 mL	milk
cayenne pepper, to taste		
salt and pepper, to taste		
½ tsp.	2 mL	dry mustard
½ cup	125 mL	freshly grated Parmesan cheese,
2 tbsp.	30 mL	finely chopped marjoram **or** oregano
12 slices	12 slices	baguette, 1 inch (2.5 cm) thick
12 slices	12 slices	cheddar cheese

In a large bowl, beat together the eggs, milk,
and seasonings. Add the mustard, cheese, and
chopped herbs; mix well. Prepare a baking
sheet or shallow ovenproof casserole dish by
coating with shortening or vegetable spray.
Dredge the baguette slices in the egg-herb
mixture and place in the baking dish. Place
a slice of cheddar cheese on each portion of
bread. Bake in the oven at 375°F (190°C) for
10 to 12 minutes. Serves 3 to 4.
Variations ✷ Use a mixture of finely
chopped herbs, such as chives, parsley, basil,
and thyme in place of the oregano or marjoram. ✷ Place 2 tsp. (10 mL) of pasta sauce on
each dredged baguette slice before topping
with cheese. ✷ Place a piece of salami or
smoked ham on each dredged baguette
slice before topping with cheese.

127

Grilled Marjoram Chicken with Tarragon Sauce

Replace the marjoram with the fresh herbs of your choice: dill, basil, thyme, sage, chives, or a mixture of these.
—John

6 6-oz.	6 180-g	boneless, skinless chicken breasts
2 tbsp.	30 mL	vegetable oil
1 tbsp.	15 mL	lime juice
6 tbsp.	90 mL	fresh marjoram
1 tsp.	5 mL	freshly ground black pepper **or** lemon pepper

Tarragon Sauce

⅔ cup	170 mL	sour cream
⅔ cup	170 mL	plain, non-fat yogourt
1 tbsp.	15 mL	lemon juice
2 tbsp.	30 mL	chopped fresh tarragon
⅓ cup	85 mL	chopped fresh chives

In a large bowl, coat the chicken breasts with oil. Add the lime juice, marjoram, and pepper; mix well. Cover and refrigerate for 2 hours. In a medium bowl, combine sauce ingredients; mix well. On the barbecue or grill at medium heat, cook the chicken for 6 to 8 minutes on each side. Serve sauce over cooked chicken or on the side. Serves 6.

Try this hearty loaf with your favourite soup.
—John

Herbed Soda Bread

Place oregano or marjoram stems on the barbecue to add a mild flavour to grilled food.

2 cups	500 mL	whole-wheat flour
2 cups	500 mL	all-purpose flour
1 tbsp.	15 mL	salt
2 tbsp.	30 mL	granulated sugar
1 tsp.	5 mL	baking soda
¾ tsp.	3.75 mL	double-acting baking powder
3 tbsp.	45 mL	butter
2 tbsp.	30 mL	chopped fresh oregano **or** marjoram
2 cups	500 mL	buttermilk

In a large bowl, sift together the flours. Add salt, sugar, baking soda, and baking powder. Work in the butter until the texture resembles a coarse meal. Add the herbs and mix evenly. Add the buttermilk and form the dough into a ball. On a floured surface, knead the dough for about 2 minutes or until dough is smooth. Line a baking sheet with parchment paper or grease the sheet with shortening. Form the dough into an 8-inch (20-cm) round and, with a sharp knife, cross the top of the loaf. Bake loaf at 375°F (190°C) for approximately 40 minutes. (The loaf should sound hollow when the base is tapped.) Cool the loaf on a wire rack. Serve warm with Herb Butter (see page 30). **Variation**❋ Replace fresh herbs with 1 tbsp. (15 mL) oregano or marjoram.

pansies, violas, & violets

Viola spp.

Hardy annuals; may self-seed.
  Pansies: Height 15 to 18 cm; spread 15 to 20 cm.
  Viola: Height 10 to 18 cm; spread 10 to 15 cm.
Perennials
  Violets: Height 10 to 15 cm; spread 20 to 25 cm.
All characterized by bicoloured and tricoloured
  flowers, in a wide range of contrasting
  shades, on dark-green foliage.

've always loved pansies! Their cheerful blooms are one of the first signs that spring has arrived. I plant a pot of pansies on the deck outside the kitchen window in mid-April so that I can see them every morning. Kissing cousins pansies, violas, and violets are all extremely hardy and can often be seen blooming half-buried in snow! ❀ I had no idea that you could eat these flowers until I saw a chef decorating a cake with pansies at the Hotel Macdonald. The soft purple petals added a dainty playfulness to the elegant icing. And the flowers taste as delicate as they look. Their mild, subtle flavour will never overpower a dish.

Try these!

Viola odorata **(sweet violet)** ❀ Wonderful perfume and sweet flavour
Viola x *wittrockiana* **(pansy)** ❀ Slight wintergreen taste
Viola tricolor **(viola)** ❀ Slight wintergreen taste

130

Planting

Start *Viola* species from seed indoors or grow from young plants purchased from a garden centre.

How much✳ Six plants; more for ornamental use.

When✳ As soon as the ground can be worked; very frost tolerant. Plant up to one month before the date of average last spring frost in your area.

Where✳ Partial shade; bright sun will produce more flowers, but hot sites will scorch plants. Prefer rich, slightly acidic, well-drained soil. Space pansies and violas 15 to 20 cm apart; space violets 10 to 15 cm apart.

Care and Nurture

Viola species are easy to grow! Do not let pansies, violas, or violets dry out: they go to seed quickly if stressed or deprived of moisture. If plants become lanky, cut them back to encourage bushiness.

These flowers are delightful in borders, mixed beds, rock gardens, cottage gardens, windowboxes, hanging baskets, and other containers.

purple 'Bingo' pansy

The other common
name for pansies—
heartsease—came
from the practice of
giving bouquets of
these flowers to people
with broken hearts.

Harvesting

Because of their excellent frost tolerance, *Violas*
will likely be both the first and the last flowers
you harvest each year.

For best flavour✽ Harvest mid-morning,
   after the dew has evaporated and before
   the day gets too hot.

Leaves✽ Edible but rarely eaten. Harvest
   small, tender violet leaves only.

Flowers✽ Gather flowers as they open. Clip
   flower stalk where it attaches to the stem, then
   cut stalk at the base of the flower head; discard
   stalk. Eat flowers whole: petals, stamens, and all.

An infusion made from
violet flowers is often
used in continental Europe
as a substitute for litmus
paper to test for acids and
bases (pH). The solution
turns red when exposed
to acids, green when
exposed to bases.

'Blueberry Cream' violets

Preserving the Harvest

Flowers will keep for several days in the fridge, but they are best used fresh. Petals can be preserved in oil, butter, or vinegar, or they can be dried and stored in a cool, dark, dry place.

Tips

* Two perennial violets, **common dog violet (*Viola riviniana*)** and **wood violet (*Viola reichenbachiana*)**, are edible. They have little fragrance but a lovely sweet flavour.

* If you're taking a summer vacation, cut back the foliage by a third and harvest flowers before you leave; when you return, you'll find another full set of blooms.

* Violets love well-rotted manure added to their soil.

* Yellow and white pansies have a gentle fragrance. That's why I often recommend using these colours in herb gardens.

* Pansies are a good choice for children's gardens because the plants are easy to grow, the flowers are reliable and colourful, and kids love the flowers because of the colourful "faces."

* Never eat the rhizomes, roots, or seed of pansies, violas, or violets.

The name "pansy" is derived from the French word *pensée,* or thought.

yellow 'Bingo' pansies

Crystallized Flowers

You can also try baby roses, scented geraniums, and orange blossoms.
—John

General information✳ Use flowers that are perfectly shaped. Wash the flowers carefully, then dry them on paper towels. Dry the flowers well in advance so they will be completely moisture-free when you start working with them. To dip flowers, leave a length of stem attached, then snip it off when you are done. Store crystallized flowers in a sealed, dry container; they will keep for up to 1 year. If any of the flowers break, they can be crushed and used for colourful confetti on desserts. (See note on flower preparation, page 24.) (Leaves can also be crystallized following these methods.)

Equipment✳ Bowl, wire rack, paint brush, fork, superfine sugar, berry sugar, or icing sugar.

Method 1✳ Make a thin paste by mixing 1 egg white with a small amount of icing sugar to form a very light foam. Brush flower petals on both sides with this mixture and sprinkle with superfine or berry sugar. Place sugared flowers on a wire rack. Air-dry for 2 hours, moving the flowers occasionally to prevent them from sticking. Place the rack on a baking sheet and put into an oven to dry completely. A gas oven with the heat from the pilot light only will be sufficient to dry the flowers. This process might take a few days. A food dehydrator on the low setting will also work.

Method 2✳ Dip the flowers in lightly beaten egg white. Dip in superfine or berry sugar. Follow the drying procedure in Method 1.

Method 3✳ Make a simple syrup of 1 cup sugar, ¼ cup water, and a pinch of cream of tartar. Bring to a boil, stirring constantly. Dip the flowers in the cooled syrup and dry on a rack. Follow the drying procedure in Method 1.

Silk and Satin Fruit with Violets

A truly delicious dessert enhanced by the colour and flavour of violets, violas, or tiny pansies. Serve in wine goblets.
—Joyce

1 19-oz. can	1 540-mL can	lychees
1	1	small pineapple
½	½	cantaloupe
½	½	honeydew
1	1	small carton strawberries
1	1	small bunch green grapes
2	2	peaches **or** nectarines
1 to 2 tbsp.	15 to 25 mL	chopped candied ginger
½ cup	125 mL	flower petals
½ cup	125 mL	cream of coconut syrup
2 tbsp.	25 mL	liquid honey
½ tsp.	2 mL	pure vanilla extract
dash	dash	salt
violets, violas, or tiny pansies		

Drain lychees and cut each one in half. Peel and cut the pineapple, cantaloupe, and honeydew into large dice. Slice the strawberries and peaches, and combine all fruit with ginger. Mix all the remaining ingredients in a saucepan and warm slightly. Cool. (Vanilla and salt greatly enhance the flavour of fruit.) Just before serving, put fruit gently into a colander to remove any collected juice (which would dilute sauce). Combine fruit with petals and sauce (see note on flower preparation, page 24). Spoon into wine goblets, garnish with matching flowers, and serve immediately. Serves 8.

Note✳ Cream of coconut syrup is purchased by the trade name *Coco Lopez* and is available in the specialty beverage supplies section of the supermarket.

Pansies, violets, and violas are all fantastic for
delicate custards, creams, jelly rolls, green salads,
and ice cream. They can also be used as colourful
garnishes, or in soups, fruit salads, or desserts. The
flowers can also be used to make tea. Violets can be
served as a garnish with meat dishes. They
complement veal dishes very nicely.

Crystallized violets may be used
for decoration on pastries,
cakes, and petit-fours.

Use chopped violet leaves in
softened butter and spread on
fish, chicken, veal, or pork.

parsley

Petroselinum crispum

Biennial or short-lived perennial; generally
grown as an annual.

Height 30 to 45 cm (Italian varieties
up to 1 m); spread to 30 cm (Italian
varieties 45 to 60 cm).

Upright, multi-stemmed plant that
forms attractive, dark-green mounds.

*We used to grow fields of parsley to
supply wholesalers. It was the prettiest crop
in the fields with its tidy, compact deep-green
foliage. It was also pest and disease free—we never
had any trouble with it. A few years ago, Evelyn Hamden,
a wonderful Lebanese lady, introduced me to tabouleh—
a salad of finely chopped parsley, tomatoes, and bulgar
wheat—and I've been enjoying it ever since. ❋Whether
you choose curled or flat-leaf varieties, parsley adds a
fresh, bright tone to food. Don't let the ubiquitous
dehydrated flakes fool you: parsley is much more
than a plate garnish!*

Try these!

Petroselinum crispum crispum **(curled parsley)**❋ Strong aroma
and flavour

Petroselinum crispum neapolitanum **(Italian parsley, flat-leaf parsley,
plain-leaf parsley)**❋ Lovely, rich, full flavour

Petroselinum crispum tuberosum **(Hamburg parsley, root parsley)**❋
Both leaves and roots are used; good for soups, stews, and steaming

Planting

Parsley is best grown from young plants purchased from a garden centre. The seed germinates very slowly and requires very warm temperatures for successful germination; the seedlings also grow very slowly.

How much✳ Two to six plants.

When✳ About a week before the date of average last spring frost in your area.

Where✳ Full sun. Prefers rich, well-drained soil. Space plants 20 to 25 cm apart.

Care and Nurture

Parsley is easy to grow! Garden parsley need little attention other than water during dry spells. Parsley grown in containers needs water every day. Parsley loves cool temperatures but will tolerate heat.

Italian parsley

curled parsley

Harvesting

Begin harvesting when parsley produces leaf stems with three segments. Harvest root parsley in the fall, when the plant is mature; pull up like parsnip.

For best flavour❋ Harvest mid-morning, after the dew has evaporated and before the day gets too hot.

Leaves❋ Harvest individual leaves by clipping the leaf stalk where it attaches to the plant stem. Cut sprigs and use whole, or strip the leaves. Stalks are edible but discard if too tough.

Flowers❋ Edible, but not normally eaten.

Preserving the Harvest

Use fresh, frozen, or dried. Keep a jar of chopped parsley in your freezer and crumble off whatever amount you need, or use the ice-cube method (see page 26). Parsley dries very well, too. Crumble dried leaves and stems and store in plastic containers.

Italian parsley

Parsley is an excellent source of vitamins A, B, and C. It is very rich in iron, iodine, and magnesium.

Parsley is an attractive ornamental, good for filling in empty spaces or edging in flower beds.

Tips

* Here's a quick and easy method for drying parsley. Dip sprigs in boiling water for 2 minutes. (I use a colander, so they're easy to get out.) Bake the sprigs on a cookie sheet in a cool oven until crisp. Keep an eye on the parsley to avoid toasting it. As soon as the leaves are cool, crush and store in an airtight container.

* Parsley prefers cooler temperatures, although it will tolerate heat. When we grew it commercially, we had little choice of location: we had to grow it in an open field! At home, I like to choose a location that is shaded from the hot late-day sun. The overall plant growth may be less vigorous, but the leaves are much sweeter and tastier.

* If parsley is left in the ground for a second season, it will flower and set seed. In warmer areas, parsley patches may sustain themselves for a few years. Plain-leaf varieties are hardier than curled varieties.

* Because of its high chlorophyll content, parsley is one of the best plants to chew to fight bad breath. I'm an advocate of eating the parsley garnish from my plate at restaurants, and I encourage my family and friends to do so too. Parsley cleanses the palate, freshens the breath, and tastes great, too! Chefs often leave a bowl of parsley sprigs in ice water in their kitchens, for the waiters to chew before serving guests in the dining room.

Parsley may irritate sensitive skin on some individuals.

Parsley gets its name from a combination of the Greek words *petros* (rock) and *selinon* (celery).

Keep a pot of curled parsley in the kitchen for easy access.

Try parsley spread with pita bread, as a vegetable dip, or on crackers and sandwiches.
—John

Spreads

Gremolata

2 cups	500 mL	Italian flat-leaf parsley
4 tbsp.	60 mL	grated lemon rind
2 tbsp.	30 mL	minced garlic

In a mixing bowl, combine all ingredients. Use immediately or refrigerate. Refrigerated in a sealed container, gremolata will keep for up to 3 months, but it is best fresh. **Hint**✷ This mixture can be frozen in small amounts to add to soups. Mix it with cream cheese or butter and serve as a spread. Use it to garnish soups, pastas, and fish. It can also be mixed with fresh bread crumbs as a seasoned coating.

Parsley Spread

2 slices	2 slices	whole-wheat bread, crusts removed, soaked in water
1 medium	1 medium	red onion, cut into large dice
3	3	garlic cloves
1 tbsp.	15 mL	sweet chili sauce
2 large bunches	2 large bunches	parsley, curly or flat-leaf, stems trimmed, coarsely chopped
3 tbsp.	45 mL	lemon juice
½ cup	125 mL	extra-virgin olive oil
3 tsp.	15 mL	balsamic vinegar
salt and ground black pepper, to taste		

Squeeze the excess water from the bread slices. Place the onions in a food processor with half the bread. Add the chili sauce, garlic, and half the parsley. Blend the mixture until it forms a smooth paste. Add the rest of the parsley, the remaining bread, half the olive oil, and 1 tbsp. (15 mL) of lemon juice. Blend again, slowly adding the remaining olive oil, lemon juice, and vinegar; mix until the mixture is smooth. Season with salt and pepper.
Yield✷ 2 cups (500ml).

Puffy and golden on the top, crunchy crisp on the bottom. Wonderful for brunch, lunch, or dinner, with lots of fried green tomatoes!
—Joyce

Quick Corn Pudding

¼ cup	50 mL	butter (for best flavour and texture)
4	4	large eggs
1 cup	250 mL	milk
1 cup	250 mL	flour
½ tsp.	2 mL	salt
¼ tsp.	1 mL	nutmeg
1 tsp.	5 mL	**each** chopped fresh thyme **and** savory
3 tbsp.	50 mL	finely chopped fresh parsley
¾ cup	175 mL	fresh **or** frozen kernel corn
2	2	green onions, finely chopped
lots of freshly ground pepper		

Heat the oven to 425°F (220°C) and get out that 9 to 10-inch (22 to 25-cm) cast-iron frying pan! Put the butter in the pan and melt in the oven. In blender or food processor, combine eggs, milk, flour, salt, and nutmeg; mix until smooth, about 2 minutes. Stir in herbs, corn, onions, and pepper. Swirl melted butter carefully around hot pan, add corn mixture, and return quickly to oven. Bake 20 to 25 minutes or until pudding is puffed, golden-brown, and crackled. Cut pudding into wedges and serve immediately with ham, pork, or chicken. Serves 6 to 8.

Deep-fry sprigs of parsley, salt immediately, and use to garnish fish or cheese dishes.

A simple parsley sauce can be made more piquant by adding lemon balm.

143

rosemary
Rosmarinus officinalis

Tender evergreen perennial; grown
 as an annual in most areas of Canada.
Height 30 to 100 cm, can reach 200 cm; spread 30 to 60 cm.
Looks like a little tree: upright bush growth habit, with
 hundreds of straight, needle-shaped, succulent
 green leaves; creeping varieties have a
 prostrate growth habit.

*At the beginning of the year, we planted a rosemary topiary to
photograph for this book. We waited, and waited, and waited…rosemary
is the very definition of a slow-growing plant! Eventually,
we gave up on the idea. Then just before Christmas, while I was
checking the poinsettias, I noticed the topiary. It was finally filled out
and gorgeous! I recently read that an American grower is raising rosemary
shrubs big enough to use as Christmas trees. That must take incredible
patience! ❋ Rosemary is a powerful herb, and a little goes a long way. Use
the tender tips for cooking, the older leaves for potpourris and sachets. Did
you know that the flowers are just as tasty as the leaves?*

Try these!
***Rosmarinus officinalis* 'Arp'** ❋ Hardier strain, survives outdoors in zone 6
 with winter protection

***Rosmarinus officinalis* 'Prostratus' (creeping rosemary)** ❋ Produces lots
 of pale-blue flowers; fine creeping/trailing growing habit

***Rosmarinus officinalis* 'Rex'** ❋ Very upright variety with large, deep-green
 leaves; vigorous growth habit

***Rosmarinus officinalis* 'Blue Boy'** ❋ Lots of flowers, excellent flavour,
 compact form; a good choice for growing indoors in small pots

Planting

Rosemary can be difficult to grow from seed. If you enjoy a challenge, start indoors from seed in February or early March; otherwise, grow young plants purchased from a garden centre or propagate from cuttings.

How much✴ At least two plants.

When✴ Around the date of the average last spring frost.

Where✴ Full sun; tolerates light shade. Excellent in containers. Prefers light, well-drained, dry soils. Space plants 45 to 60 cm apart in the garden; space 1 plant per pot in a small container, 3 to 5 in a large container.

Care and Nurture

Once established, rosemary is easy to grow! Young plants need lots of water, but established rosemary is drought tolerant and can take a dry spell or two.

Harvesting

If you bring your rosemary inside for the winter and put it in a sunny window, you can continue to enjoy fresh leaves year-round. Harvest sparingly during the winter, however, because the plant gets less light and produces fewer leaves.

For best flavour✴ Harvest leaves just before the flowers bloom.

Leaves✴ Harvest throughout the growing season. Cut sprigs and use whole, or strip the needles and discard the stem.

Flowers✴ Harvest as they open. Clip cleanly from the stem. Remove any green bits before eating.

Preserving the Harvest

Rosemary leaves are best preserved by drying. The flowers can be used fresh or preserved in oil.

Tips

✴ If rosemary is hardy in your area, remember that it's a short-lived perennial. After a few years it will become bare, sparse, and woody. I like to replace my plant every 3 years. Never cut it back in the fall: the growth above the ground will help protect and insulate the roots over the winter.

*You can make this recipe with
dried herbs instead of fresh, but
use only half the amounts listed.*
—John

Herbed Focaccia

1 cup	250 mL	warm water
1 package (¼ oz.)	7.5 g	active dry yeast
1 tsp.	5 mL	honey
2½ to 3 cups	625 to 750 mL	all-purpose flour
1 tsp.	5 mL	salt
3 tbsp.	15 mL	extra-virgin olive oil
½ tsp.	2.5 mL	chopped fresh rosemary
½ tsp.	2.5 mL	chopped fresh basil
½ tsp.	2.5 mL	chopped fresh thyme
½ tsp.	2.5 mL	chopped fresh oregano
1 tbsp.	15 mL	cornmeal
coarse salt for sprinkling		

In a large bowl, mix together the warm water,
yeast, and honey. Add 1 cup (250 mL) of flour and
beat the mixture with a whisk until it is smooth
and creamy. Cover the mixture with plastic wrap
and let rest for 5 minutes at room temperature.
Add to the rested mixture 2 tbsp. (30 mL) of olive
oil, the chopped herbs, and another 1 cup (250
mL) of flour. Mix together for 3 minutes or until
the dough is smooth. Add the remaining flour
until the dough forms a soft, sticky ball. Turn the
dough out on a lightly floured surface and knead
for 3 minutes. Coat a baking sheet with non-stick
spray and sprinkle with cornmeal. Shape the
dough into a round loaf and brush with remaining
olive oil; sprinkle lightly with coarse salt. Cover
the loaf with an inverted bowl or kitchen towel
and let rest in a warm place for 10 minutes. Bake
at 400°F (200°C) for 20 to 25 minutes or until
golden-brown. Cool on a wire rack.

146

A delicious variation of refrigerator pickles to prepare for your family and as Christmas hostess gifts!
—Joyce

All-Season Zesty Zucchini-Rosemary Pickles

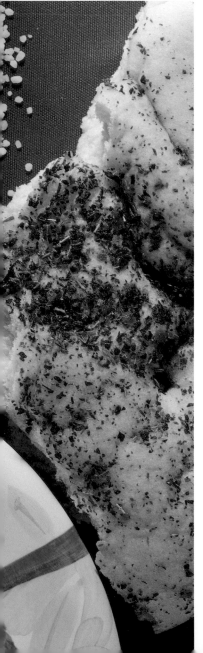

3 6-inch	3 15-cm	zucchini
1	1	large red or sweet onion
2 tsp.	10 mL	pickling salt
2	2	red bell peppers
2 cups	500 mL	vinegar
⅔ cup	150 mL	sugar
2 tbsp.	25 mL	pickling spice in spice bag or tea ball
1 or 2	1 or 2	jalapeño peppers (optional)
3	3	long sprigs rosemary

Wash zucchini thoroughly and cut off ends. Thinly slice zucchini and onion. Mix the zucchini and onion thoroughly with salt and let stand 30 minutes. Rinse and drain. Meanwhile, seed and thinly slice the red peppers (or for extra colour, use small red, yellow, and green peppers). Combine vinegar, sugar, and pickling spice; cover and gently simmer for 5 minutes. Remove spice ball. Add all vegetables immediately (with 1 or 2 jalapeños if desired). Stir, cover tightly, remove from heat, and allow to cool. Pack into a clean jar (a recycled pickle jar is great). Blanch the rosemary in boiling water until it turns brilliant green, about 30 seconds; immediately plunge into ice water. With a fork, work the rosemary down the sides of the jar. Refrigerate. Pickles may be used within 24 hours but will retain great flavour and texture for up to 2 months.
Yield ✱ 4 cups (1 litre).
Note ✱ During the winter season, supermarkets carry the perfect size of zucchini for making these super pickles.

Enjoy this tangy combination year-round!
—John

Tomato-Rosemary Barbecued Ribs

Rosemary is so rich in essential oils that it will keep its flavour longer than most herbs, often as long as 2 or 3 years.

⅔ cup	170 mL	vegetable oil
½ cup	125 mL	tomato paste
1 tbsp.	15 mL	tomato ketchup
4 tbsp.	60 mL	apple-cider vinegar
1 cup	250 mL	orange juice
2 tbsp.	30 mL	chopped fresh rosemary leaves
or		
1 tbsp.	15 mL	dried rosemary leaves
4 lbs.	1.8 kg	pork, beef short, or cross ribs

Rosemary complements the taste of cantaloupe, grapefruit, strawberries, and oranges. It is also good with cheese.

Prepare marinade by stirring together oil, tomato paste, ketchup, vinegar, orange juice, and rosemary; set aside. Trim any excess fat from the ribs. In a large saucepan, boil enough lightly salted water to cover the ribs. Put ribs in the water and reduce heat to simmer; simmer ribs for 30 minutes. Drain well. Place ribs in a large bowl or large glass dish. Pour the marinade over ribs, coating them well. Marinate for 8 hours in the refrigerator. Barbecue at low heat and cook the ribs slowly, turning frequently, 40 to 45 minutes. If baking, turn oven to 350°F (175°C)and bake ribs in a single layer on a foil-lined baking sheet. Turn the ribs until they are dark brown and crisp, about 30 to 35 minutes. Use extra marinade to baste while cooking.

Variation❋ Replace ribs with 6 skinless, boneless chicken breasts. Cook on barbecue for 10 to 12 minutes on each side or bake in oven at 350°F (175°C) for 10 to 12 minutes on each side.

Drop a sprig of rosemary into the oil or butter used for sautéing to add a subtle flavour to the food. You can also put a sprig of rosemary in a pot of boiled new potatoes to add an excellent flavour.

Potato Cakes with Rosemary

Use Russets or Burbank potatoes for this recipe because they have a high starch content with low moisture and sugar content. The batter can also be formed into individual pancakes, if you prefer.
—John

Use rosemary stems as barbecue skewers.

3 lbs.	1.5 kg	potatoes, cooked and shredded
salt and ground black pepper, to taste		
2 tsp.	30 mL	finely chopped fresh rosemary
1	1	egg, beaten
¼ cup	60 mL	butter
¼ cup	60 mL	vegetable oil

Wash and scrub the potatoes. Put the potatoes in a large saucepan with enough water to cover them; cook them gently until they are firm in the centre, about 20 minutes. Drain the potatoes and let them cool. Remove the peel. Through the large holes of a grater, shred the potatoes into a bowl. Season with salt and pepper; add the rosemary and the beaten egg. Mix well. Melt the butter and oil together in a small saucepan. Heat a large skillet over medium heat; add half the oil and butter. Add the potatoes in an even layer; compress lightly with the back of a spatula. Cook for 3 to 4 minutes, until a crust forms and the bottom is light brown. Invert the cake onto a large dinner plate. Add the remaining oil and butter to the skillet and slide the cake gently back into the pan. Cook the underside of the cake until it forms a brown crust, about 5 minutes. Turn the cake onto a platter and cut into wedges. Serve immediately with sour cream.

Variation✳ Dill, oregano, and thyme work equally well with this recipe. Dry herbs can be substituted for fresh, but use about half the amount called for.

roses
Rosa spp.

Perennials of variable hardiness.
Height and spread vary widely, depending on species.
Shrub, featuring fragrant blossoms on graceful green
    stems with dark-green leaves.

oses are legendary ornamental plants,

bringing joy and inspiration to countless millions of people.

They are also wonderful edible flowers. I've probably eaten

thousands of rosehips over the years. My mother and my aunt

insisted that eating rosehips kept them healthy, and I believe them.

We used to pick hips wild or right from Mom's garden, eating them like

apples, savouring the thin layer of flesh. I still enjoy rosehips, but now

I also sprinkle rose petals over many foods, a touch that makes

a festive meal special. ✻ If a rose smells good, the petals will

taste good. All rose petals are edible, and each variety

tastes slightly different. Experiment to find your favourites.

Try these!
Species roses (*Rosa rugosa*) are best for crops of rosehips, because
    they produce lots of edible pulp. **Old garden roses** or **antique roses
    (*Rosa alba, Rosa damascena, Rosa gallica*)** are known for their beautiful,
    fragrant flowers. Please see *Lois Hole's Rose Favorites* for specific variety
    recommendations.

Planting

Plant large, well-rooted, container-grown roses from the garden centre.

How much ❋ One plant of each type you enjoy.

When ❋ Anytime during the growing season—from early spring to just before freeze-up.

Where ❋ Full sun. Demands rich, well-drained soil. Space variable, depending on variety.

Care and Nurture

Roses are easy to grow! Try this basic advice: water once a week, fertilize once a month, prune once a year, and deadhead once in a while. Roses need more water than most plants. As a rule of thumb, give each rose 5 L of water per week for every 30 cm of height. Water only around the base of the plant to reduce the incidence of powdery mildew disease. Cut off damaged or diseased branches whenever you spot them. Fertilize once a month with 28-14-14 rose food. Use a fertilizer with chelated iron added to avoid veiny leaves. Ensure that the plants are well watered before freeze-up. For more-detailed care and nurture instructions, see *Lois Hole's Rose Favorites*.

The best tasting rose is *Rosa rugosa alba*; other *rugosa* roses are delicious, too. Use them in jams, syrups, ice cream, or salads. The petals from French roses (*Rosa gallica*) make an excellent addition as an edible garnish in salads. They have a spicy fragrance.

Harvesting

For a lovely blend of flavours, pull a few petals from several different types of roses and combine. The darkest petals are said to be most flavourful.

During World War Two, soldiers and children alike ate rosehips for their high vitamin C content.

For best flavour✽ Harvest mid-morning, after the dew has evaporated and before the day gets too hot.

Leaves✽ Not harvested.

Flowers✽ Just as the flowers open fully, well before they start to fade. Cut stem ten to twelve centimetres from base of flower; remove stem and greenery when you're ready to use the petals.

Hips✽ Pick when they are red and plump, but not soft and overripe. Pull cleanly from the plant.

Preserving the Harvest

It was once a custom to hang a rose over the dinner table to signify that all discussions were to remain confidential.

Petals should be used fresh. Wash the petals and remove the green or white heel at the base of each one. The petals may be preserved in butter, syrup, or vinegar or they may be crystallized. Prepare hips quickly after harvesting by slicing off the stem and blossom ends, cutting the hips in half, and scooping out the fibres and seeds with a spoon. The halves can be eaten fresh or dried on a screen in a shady, well-ventilated room.

Tips

Shakespeare and his contemporaries consumed rose petals in everything from teas to jellies.

✽ I like to plant several varieties that bloom at different times of the season, so I have a continuous supply of flower petals.

If a rose smells good, it will taste good.

Create colourful, mildly flavoured
butters with chopped flower petals.
—John

Flower Butter

Rose Butter

½ lb.	225 g	unsalted butter
1 tbsp.	15 mL	icing sugar **or** granulated sugar
2 tbsp.	30 mL	rose petals
1 to 2 drops	1 to 2 drops	almond extract, vanilla extract, **or** rosewater

In a medium bowl, soften the butter with
a spatula or wooden spoon. Wash and thoroughly dry the petals; with a sharp knife,
chop them finely (see note on flower preparation, page 24). Add the petals, sugar, and
flavouring to the butter and incorporate
evenly. Store in the freezer. Wrapped and
sealed, rose butter will keep for 2 to 3 weeks.

Flower-Petal Butters

1 lb.	454 g	unsalted butter
½ cup	125 mL	chopped flower petals

In a large bowl, soften the butter with a
spatula or wooden spoon. Add the petals
and other ingredients as desired (see variations
below). Form the butter into attractive shapes
on a baking sheet. Freeze for 2 hours. Remove the butter shapes from tray and store
in sealed, labelled plastic bags.

Variations ❋ Add any of these flavours to the
recipe above, or try your own combinations!
2 tbsp. (30 mL) icing sugar (for sweet butters);
2 tbsp. (30 mL) lemon juice and 2 tsp. (10 mL)
grated lemon rind; 2 tbsp. (30 mL) lime juice
and 2 tsp. (10 mL) grated lime rind; 2 to 3 tsp.
(10 to 15 mL) pure vanilla essence, orange
essence, almond essence, or rosewater.

Hint ❋ Salted butter can be used but choose
the lightly salted type.

Hint ❋ Serve flower-petal butters with sweet
biscuits, muffins, waffles and pancakes, grilled
fish, and cooked carrots and turnips.

Garnish this dessert with rose petals and candied ginger; serve with whipped cream.
—John

Gingered Rose Custard

4	4	medium egg yolks
pinch	pinch	salt
⅓ cup	85 mL	granulated sugar
2 cups	500 mL	heavy cream
6 slices	6 slices	fresh ginger root
½ tsp.	2.5 mL	rosewater
2 tbsp.	30 mL	sweet sherry

In a large bowl, beat the egg yolks with an electric mixer; add a pinch of salt and continue beating until yolks are a pale-lemon colour. In a medium saucepan over medium heat, warm the ginger slices and heavy cream. Do not boil. With a slotted spoon, remove the ginger slices; add the rosewater. Pour the flavoured cream over the egg yolks and mix well. Over a double boiler, cook the custard mix, stirring constantly, until it thickens and coats the back of a spoon. Add the sherry and cool the custard over an ice-water bath. Pour the custard into serving dishes.
Yield ❈ 4 to 6 servings.

Rose petals may be used as a topping for a variety of fruit pies. The petals should be placed on top of the fruit before placing the pastry top.

155

sage

Salvia officinalis

Hardy perennial.

Height 45 to 60 cm; spread to 1 m.

Herb with woolly, pebbled, oval grey-green or variegated leaves and blue, purple, pink, or white flowers.

My mother used sage often, especially for chicken and turkey dressings. I remember her cautioning me how much sage to add from the jar she kept on the counter. "Be careful, it's strong. Don't use too much," she would say. Today I cook with sage regularly, but I always remember her warning. ❋ Sage is a valuable culinary herb as it aids in digesting fatty foods, both savoury and sweet. The flavour of sage flowers varies, so sample a few before cooking with them. Although pineapple and clary sage flowers can be subtle and sweet, regular sage flowers can be pungent.

Try these!

***Salvia officinalis* (garden sage)** ❋ Most commonly grown; the main culinary variety

***Salvia officinalis purpurea* (purple sage)** ❋ Very aromatic purple foliage; excellent in stuffings, omelettes, soups, and stews; requires winter protection to survive

***Salvia officinalis* 'Tricolor' (tricolour sage)** ❋ Aromatic foliage; mild flavour; very decorative; tender perennial—requires winter protection to survive

***Salvia elegans* [aka *S. rutilans*] (pineapple sage)** ❋ Tender perennial; very sweet, vibrant red flowers

pineapple sage

Planting

Sage is best grown from young plants
purchased from a garden centre.

How much✳ At least two plants.

When✳ Two weeks after the date of the
average last spring frost.

Where✳ Full sun, sheltered; will tolerate
light shade. Grows well in containers.
Prefers rich, well-drained soil. Space
plants 30 to 45 cm apart.

Care and Nurture

Sage requires some care to grow well.
Never overwater. Prune lightly in July,
after flowering, to encourage new growth.
Sage bushes are short-lived perennials; they
get woody, produce less foliage, and begin
to die out after 3 or 4 years. I like to replace
my plant with new stock after 3 years. In
cooler climates, mulch lightly in the fall
to protect plants from winter's chill.

Sage was first cultivated by the ancient Greeks, who
valued it as a medicinal plant. Sage has long been
purported to possess great healing properties; a
proverb from the Middle Ages goes, "Why should
a man die if sage flourishes in his garden?"

Berggarten sage

golden sage

Harvesting

Harvest leaves regularly to encourage new growth. The younger leaves have a better flavour.

For best flavour✻ Harvest leaves before the flowers open.

Leaves✻ Harvest *S. officinalis* throughout the season, up to early fall. Harvest individual leaves by clipping the leaf stalk where it attaches to the plant stem. Cut sprigs and use whole, or strip the leaves. Discard tough stalks.

Flowers✻ Harvest *S. elegans* flowers as they open. Clip cleanly from the stem. Remove any green bits before eating.

Preserving the Harvest

Dry sage leaves slowly to preserve their flavour; they take a long time to dry, but once they are thoroughly dry, they will keep for about a year. Use flowers fresh or preserve in vinegar. Pineapple sage flowers are best crystallized— the red flowers are very pretty.

For an unusual window box, combine different varieties of sage.

The Romans considered sage a sacred herb and gathered it with ceremony.
A sacrifice of bread and wine was made, and the gatherer wore
a white tunic, feet bared and washed. The sage was never cut with an
iron tool—a good idea, since iron salts are not compatible with sage.

Purple sage leaves have a lovely colour and texture.

Tips

* Here are some other edible sage varieties you may want to try.

  ***Salvia officinalis* 'Berggarten'** * Low-growing plant with extra-large leaves; one of the best-known choice strains.

  ***Salvia officinalis aurea* (golden sage)** * Very pretty chartreuse-yellow leaves; same flavour as standard sage.

  ***Salvia officinalis* 'Holt's Mammoth'** * Tall plant with extra-large leaves; a well-known choice strain.

* Clary sage (*Salvia sclarea*), an annual sage grown for its aromatic flowers, which may be blue, purple, mauve, or cream-coloured, has great ornamental value. We sell it as a bedding plant, and although it's not our most popular annual, there are customers who ask for it year after year to plant in their flower beds.

tricolour sage

common sage

159

Excellent with salads, grilled meats, and barbecued meats.
—John

Buttermilk Corn Muffins with Sage

1½ cups	375 mL	all-purpose flour
1½ cups	375 mL	yellow cornmeal
1 tbsp.	15 mL	baking powder
1 tbsp.	15 mL	granulated sugar
1 tsp.	5 mL	salt
1 tsp.	5 mL	baking soda
1½ cups	375 mL	buttermilk
5 tbsp.	75 mL	melted shortening
3	3	eggs
3 tbsp.	45 mL	fresh sage leaves, finely chopped
or		
1 tbsp.	15 mL	dried sage

Line or spray 12 3-inch (7.5-cm) muffin cups. In a large bowl, sift together flour, cornmeal, baking powder, sugar, salt, and baking soda. In a separate, medium-sized bowl, mix together the buttermilk, melted shortening, and eggs. Add the chopped sage to the liquid mixture; incorporate well. Stir liquid mixture into dry ingredients until just combined. Don't overmix. Fill muffin tins three-quarters full with batter. Bake at 425°F (220°C) until the muffins are golden-brown, about 20 to 25 minutes. Serve warm with Herb Butter (see page 30).

Scatter sage flowers over a green salad. The flowers can also be infused to make a lightly flavoured tea.

Easy and delicious! Serve with lemongrass rice or noodles and Herb Butter (see page 30).
—John

Shrimp with Sage

3 tbsp.	45 mL	vegetable oil
2 tbsp.	30 mL	lemon juice
salt and lemon pepper, to taste		
24	24	large shrimp, peeled and deveined
18	18	fresh sage leaves

In a medium bowl, whisk together oil, lemon juice, salt, and pepper. Add the shrimp to the bowl and toss; marinate for 10 minutes. Wash and pat dry the sage leaves. Thread shrimp on wood or metal skewers (soak wood skewers for 30 minutes first to prevent burning). Use 4 shrimp per skewer, each shrimp separated by a sage leaf. Cook the shrimp on the grill in a skillet over medium heat or on the barbecue, 4 to 5 minutes each side. Don't overcook!

Hint ✺ Doneness is a time-sensitive process; it's better to undercook than overcook. Dry heat, such as the grill or barbecue, tends to dry food more than most other cooking procedures.

Hint ✺ Fresh or frozen shrimp are equally good in this recipe—the quality is usually consistent. I prefer to buy them frozen, headless, with the shell on. Shrimp are purchased by count per pound, e.g., 21 to 25 per pound, 26 to 30 per pound. The higher the number, the more (smaller) shrimp per pound. Frozen shrimp can be easily defrosted in cold water.

Breads seasoned with sage add an excellent flavour to sandwiches made with pork, turkey, or chicken.

A richly flavoured pork roast usually found only in European restaurants.
—Joyce

Roast Pork with Garlic, Sage, and Madeira

4 lb.	2 kg	pork roast
fresh garlic		
lemon pepper		
chives		
4 tbsp.	50 mL	chopped fresh sage
2 tbsp.	25 mL	chopped fresh marjoram
2 tbsp.	25 mL	chopped fresh thyme
3 tbsp.	50 mL	chopped fresh celery leaves
¼ cup	50 mL	Madeira, dry sherry, **or** apple juice

Cut shallow diagonal lines across top and bottom of roast. Rub thoroughly with garlic and lemon pepper. Place a bed of chives on the roasting pan. Combine the chopped herbs and put one-third of the mixture on the chives; lay the roast on the bed of chives. Work the remaining herbs into the cut areas on the top of the roast. Enclose the roast tightly in foil and place in a 325°F (160°C) oven for 1 hour. Remove foil, pour Madeira over roast, and cook for an additional 1½ to 2 hours or until pork registers 180°F (90°C) on a meat thermometer. Serve with chilled chunky applesauce, garlic mashed potatoes, and fresh green beans or summer squash. Serves 4 to 6.

Fried Sage Leaves

24	24	fresh sage leaves
⅓ cup	85 mL	seasoned flour
salt and sugar, to taste, for seasoning		
oil for deep frying		

Wash and dry the sage leaves. Dust the leaves
with seasoned flour. Heat frying oil to 350°F
(180°C). Fry the leaves 4 or 5 at a time for
1 minute. Remove the leaves with a slotted
spoon or skimmer and drain on paper towel.
Sprinkle the leaves with salt and sugar.
Serve immediately.

*Large leaves are best for this
recipe. Scented varieties of sage
—tricolour, purple, golden,
pineapple—would be fine.
—John*

savory

Satureia hortensis (summer savory), *Satureia montana* (winter savory)

Summer savory: Annual.

Winter savory: Hardy evergreen perennial.

Summer savory: Height 30 to 45 cm; spread 30 to 60 cm.
Large, widely branched bush with long, lance-shaped leaves
and pink or white flowers.

Winter savory: Height 15 to 40 cm; spread 15 to 30 cm.
Compact, low-growing bush with lance-shaped
leaves and white or pink flowers.

The savories are often overlooked, but they offer a pleasant change from some of our more common herbs. I like to sprinkle chopped summer savory on broad beans. (I also put some sprigs in the pot with fresh beans when I steam them.) Broad beans, a traditional English dish, are one of my husband Ted's favourite vegetables, and the fresh herbs add a special touch to this simple dish. ❋ Summer savory has a strong, peppery, marjoram- or thyme-like flavour, well suited to pea, bean, and lentil dishes. Winter savory is stronger and more pungent, complementing game meats and patés.

Try these!

Satureia hortensis (**summer savory**) ❋ Easiest to grow; delicate flavour

Satureia montana (**winter savory**) ❋ Strong, pungent flavour

Satureia biflora (**lemon savory**) ❋ Tender perennial with an intense
lemon scent and flavour; rare, often difficult to locate

Planting

Savory can be started indoors from seed, grown from young plants purchased from a garden centre, or split from an established plant early in the spring.

How much❋ At least two plants.

When❋ Two weeks after the date of the average last spring frost.

Where❋ Full sun to light shade. Prefers light, well-drained soil. Space plants 30 cm apart.

Care and Nurture

Savory is easy to grow! Let the soil surface dry before you water, then soak thoroughly. Feed lightly. Winter savory should be divided and replanted every 2 or 3 years. Do this in the early spring by digging up the clump and removing any of the old, tough growth in the centre. Then split the balance of the plant into smaller clumps and replant.

Harvesting

Summer savory tends to get leggy, so don't hesitate to cut it back hard (by up to a third) to keep it producing. Harvest winter savory regularly to keep it looking bushy and full.

For best flavour❋ Harvest summer savory in late spring or early summer, before the plant flowers—later than that, the taste gets somewhat bitter. Winter savory can be harvested all season long, but young leaves taste best.

Leaves❋ Harvest individual leaves by clipping the leaf stalk where it attaches to the plant stem. Cut sprigs and use whole, or strip the leaves. Discard tough stalks.

Flowers❋ Edible, but not normally eaten; collect in late summer.

Preserving the Harvest

Summer savory is best preserved by drying. Winter savory can be dried or frozen.

Tips

❋ The leaves should be gathered before the plant flowers. I like to cut my plants back by about two-thirds after flowering and use the new, fresh, sweet shoots.

❋ Trim winter savory back in the spring to encourage new growth.

❋ I also like to prune my summer savory in the spring, about a month after I set the young plants into the garden. Summer savory grows vigorously and can get quite lanky. Pruning soon after the plants are established encourages bushy, more compact plants.

summer savory

I like to use the "softer" herbs (e.g., thyme, basil, marjoram, tarragon, mint, and dill) for flavoured mayonnaises.
—John

Savory Mayonnaise

1 cup	250 mL	mayonnaise **or** light mayonnaise
2 tbsp.	30 mL	chopped savory

Blend ingredients until savory is well incorporated. If you like, add up to 2 tsp. (10 mL) of lemon juice or flavoured vinegar to freshen up the flavour. Make flavoured mayonnaise in small batches and refrigerate; it will keep for 2 weeks.

Hint✳ Uses for herbed mayonnaise: Try as a sandwich and canapé spread, in vegetable dips, as a cold sauce for poached and grilled fish, and in vegetable salads and pasta salads. Try stirring a spoonful into cold vegetable soup!

Variation✳ Substitute 2 tbsp. (30mL) of finely chopped basil, dill, oregano, tarragon, or thyme for the savory.

Savory is often used in pasta, stuffings, pork pies, stews, soups, and sausages. It is also one of the herbs added to poultry seasoning. It is particularly tasty used in combination with lemon pepper and German mustard and makes a nice addition to a bouquet garni. Savory can even improve those boxed macaroni-and-cheese dinners!

Scrumptious served with baked chicken, meat loaf, or broiled fish!
—Joyce

Cheese Mashed Potatoes with Savory

4 to 6	4 to 6	medium potatoes
milk		
butter		
½ cup	125 mL	grated old cheddar cheese
1 tbsp.	15 mL	finely chopped savory
3	3	green onions, chopped
pepper **or** lemon pepper		

Cook potatoes in a small amount of salted water until soft. Use a good "mashing" variety of potato such as Netted Gem or Yukon Gold. Drain thoroughly and shake pan over high heat to remove all moisture. Mash lightly, then add a small amount of warmed milk and butter. Mash until light and fluffy, but not too long or potatoes will become gelatinous. Stir in cheese, savory, and onions. Season to taste with freshly ground pepper. Cover tightly and keep warm for 3 to 5 minutes to melt cheese and combine flavours. Serves 4 to 5.
Variation✽ For a great variation, cook some carrots and cauliflower with potatoes.
Hint✽ Leftovers make a delicious base for making fish patties, especially tuna.

Add savory to cookies, short bread, spice cake, and corn bread. It can also be added to jelly.

167

sorrel

Rumex acetosa

Hardy perennial.
Height 30 to 150 cm; spread 25 to 45 cm.
**Distinguished by pale-green stems and thick,
    long-stalked leaves.**

I was unfamiliar with this herb until one of our German customers, upon learning of my ignorance, said in a shocked voice, "You don't know of sorrel? You must have sorrel!" The best tips often come from my customers, so I dutifully tried some and now I wouldn't be without it. But I've found that sorrel is one of those "love it or hate it" herbs—there's no in-between. ✹ *I love to nibble on sorrel leaves! I tend to snack on the plants as I walk through the greenhouse. They're succulent and juicy—tangy, zesty, and slightly acidic—and taste great both on their own and in soups, salads, and other dishes.*

Try these!

Rumex acetosa **(common sorrel)** ✹ Mild flavour; large, long leaves

Rumex scutatus **(true French sorrel)** ✹ More concentrated flavour;
    smaller leaf

Planting

Seed sorrel directly into the garden as soon as the ground is workable or, to get a jump on the season, set out young plants purchased from a garden centre.

How much❋ Two or three plants.

When❋ Around the date of the average last spring frost.

Where❋ Full sun. Prefers moist, well-drained soil. Space plants 60 cm apart.

Care and Nurture

Sorrel is very easy to grow! Once established, water during periods of dry weather. Remove flower spikes as soon as they appear to encourage leaf production. Divide and replant sorrel every 3 to 4 years, or when the plants get crowded. Early spring is the best time to do this, just as the plants are emerging. Sorrel requires little fertilizer.

Harvesting

Once sorrel is established, you can harvest leaves right through to autumn: sorrel is quite frost tolerant. To keep the leaves mild and tender, remove any flowers before they open: the leaves get very bitter after the plant has flowered.

For best flavour❋ Harvest young, tender, juicy leaves: older leaves can have a sharp, sometimes bitter, flavour.

Leaves❋ Clip leaf stalks where they attach to the main plant; discard any tough stems.

Flowers❋ Edible, but not normally eaten.

Preserving the Harvest

Dried sorrel has little flavour. Use sorrel fresh or freeze it.

Tips

❋ Sorrel contains oxalic acid, which should be avoided by individuals with gout, rheumatism, and kidney problems.

❋ Sorrel requires minimal care and attention beyond watering. I like to give my plants a good shot of 20-20-20 after I cut them back severely. This creates a fresh flush of tender, young leaves.

A hearty summer soup. Try it with crusty bread and Herb Butter (see page 30).
—John

Sorrel Soup

2 tbsp.	30 mL	butter
1	1	medium onion, cut into small dice
2	2	garlic cloves, crushed
1 cup	250 mL	chopped sorrel leaves
2 10-oz. cans	2 284-mL cans	chicken bouillon
1	1	bay leaf
4	4	medium potatoes, peeled, cubed, and cooked
salt and white pepper, to taste		
1 cup	250 mL	heavy cream
chopped parsley and chives, for garnish		

In a medium saucepan, melt the butter over medium heat. Add the diced onion, garlic, and sorrel. Stir the mixture until the onion is soft but not brown, 3 to 4 minutes. Add the chicken bouillon and bay leaf; bring to a boil, stirring occasionally. Reduce heat to low, cover, and cook for 20 minutes. Add the potatoes and cook, uncovered, for 5 minutes. Season the soup and remove the bay leaf. In a small bowl, temper the cream with some of the hot broth. Over low heat, add the cream to the soup; **do not boil.** Adjust seasoning and garnish soup with chopped parsley and chives.

Hint❋ Tempering means to add some of the hot liquid to the cream to equalize the temperature before adding it to the cooking pot. If the cream is added cold, it may separate.

Hint❋ This soup freezes well. Do not boil when re-heating!

Hint❋ Light cream could be used in place of heavy cream.

Thinly sliced green tomatoes are a great addition—tart and tangy, somewhat like lemongrass.
—Joyce

Summer Stir-Fry with Sorrel

2 cups	500 mL	cherry tomatoes
2 cups	500 mL	sliced zucchini
1 cup	250 mL	snow peas
6	6	green onions, sliced
8	8	large sorrel leaves, slivered
seasoned salt, to taste		
lemon pepper, to taste		

Pour a small amount of water or oil into a frying pan. Add tomatoes, zucchini, snow peas, and onions. Stir-fry 1 to 2 minutes or until barely heated through. Remove from heat, add remaining ingredients, and stir until the sorrel wilts. Serve immediately. Serves 4. Excellent with rice and fish or chicken. Also tasty with a light pasta or macaroni and cheese on a rainy day!

Sorrel should be cooked only briefly to preserve its fresh flavour.

Fresh, young leaves can be added to salads, sauces, soups, cream cheeses, and egg dishes.

sunflowers
Helianthus annuus

Annual.

Height 30 cm to 2 m (some varieties can
grow to heights of 6 m or more);
spread 15 to 45 cm.

Huge flower heads sport bright-yellow
petals around a centre of black seeds.

*W*hen I was a little girl,
it seemed that every farmer in
Saskatchewan grew sunflowers.
I used to carry around the mature flower
heads and eat the seeds like popcorn. I got
pretty good at cracking the shells and spitting
them out so that I could munch on the delicious seed
within—in fact, I even won a couple of spitting contests!

❋ *Sunflower seeds are a delicious snack, and sprouted seeds
make an excellent addition to salads and sandwiches. The
petals have the same nutty flavour as the seeds and can be
added to baked bread or salads. The flower buds can be eaten
whole; they taste much like Jerusalem artichokes.*

Try it!

***Helianthus annuus* (sunflower)** ❋ Large-seeded, tall-growing sunflowers;
some varieties may reach heights of 5 m, but most will grow 2 to 3 m

Sunflowers are wonderful in backgrounds, borders, and hedges. They're also a great choice for children's gardens because the seeds are large enough for little fingers to handle and the plants come up quickly and are easily maintained.

Planting

Seed sunflowers directly into the garden or, to get a jump on the season, set out young plants purchased from a garden centre. If you use young plants, be sure they come in individually celled containers: sunflowers don't like to have their roots disturbed.

How much✱ Two to three plants; more for ornamental use.

When✱ Seed as soon as the soil can be worked. Set out young plants one week after the date of the average last spring frost.

Where✱ Full sun. Prefers rich, well-drained soil; will grow in any soil. Space tall varieties 60 cm apart; space short varieties 45 to 50 cm apart.

Care and Nurture

Sunflowers are very easy to grow! Rain generally provides all the moisture they require, but if conditions are dry, additional watering will produce larger, lusher plants and bigger flowers. Sunflowers self-sow readily, so don't be surprised if a few plants keep turning up year after year, either in your own yard or your neighbour's.

The name *Helianthus* is derived from the Greek words *helios* (sun) and *anthos* (flower). Sunflowers are heliotropic, meaning that they follow the sun. The flowers and leaves turn to the rising sun in the east and follow it across the sky.

Harvesting

The flower buds, ray petals, and dried seeds can be eaten. If you're growing sunflowers for the flower buds, choose a perennial or multi-stemmed annual variety, rather than a single-stem annual variety: they produce lots of flower heads. If you're growing them for the seeds, choose a single-stem variety and don't harvest petals from the flower heads.

For best flavour✻ Pampered sunflowers will produce the best growth.

Leaves✻ Not harvested.

Flowers✻ Harvest buds as they appear. Clip buds cleanly from stem. Once the flower opens, use only the petals. Pull individual ray petals from growing flower heads, or cut whole flowers and strip the ray petals. Discard the central disc florets.

Seeds✻ Cut the mature flower heads of sunflowers when they droop, the back of the head is dry and brown, and the seeds are dark and dry. Brush off any remaining petals with your fingers.

Boil sunflower petals to make a yellow dye. Sunflower is a good bee plant as it gives the hives large quantities of wax and nectar.

On a warm day, a large sunflower consumes 17 times as much water as a person.

Preserving the Harvest

Use the petals and flower buds fresh—they do not store well. I like to tie the mature sunflower heads to the beams of my garage until I'm ready to use them. It's cool and dry there, and the heads get lots of air movement, preventing decay.

Tips

* Grow small varieties in containers. Ikarus and Soraya look great in large containers; you can also try Pacino, Big Smile, and Teddy Bear (my favourite, since its flowers looks like those in the Van Gogh painting).

Tall Mammoth sunflowers have heads up to 40 cm across, containing 2000 seeds.

* Perennial sunflowers tend to deplete the soil where they grow. They should be replanted in a new site every few years, with plenty of well-rotted manure and compost added to the new spot. I prefer to add lots of well-rotted manure and compost each fall so I don't have to move my plants. Instead, I divide the plant every 3 or 4 years. Perennial sunflowers tolerate poor soil but they don't like to dry out.

* Once, some farmers who lived down the road from us planted sunflowers close to their corn. Unfortunately, crows swooped down and devastated both crops. To prevent birds from eating all the seeds before you harvest them, cover the flower heads with brown paper bags as soon as they mature.

* The best fertilizers for sunflowers contain twice as much potassium as nitrogen, e.g., 15-15-30.

Sunflower seeds are a popular and common snack food enjoyed by millions of people worldwide. Sunflower seeds are used in Russia and Portugal to make a nutritious whole-grain bread. Large-scale cultivation of sunflowers began in Russia, where sunflower seeds are now sold on street corners.

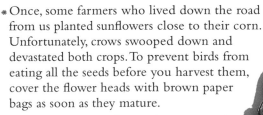

Pumpkin-Sunflower Bread

A delicious blend of fall flavours.
—John

1 tbsp.	15mL	active dry yeast
¾ cup	175 mL	warm water
1 tbsp.	15 mL	honey
1 cup	250 mL	pumpkin purée
2 tsp.	10 mL	coarse salt
2 tbsp.	30 mL	soft unsalted butter
3½ to 4 cups	825 to 1000 mL	bread flower or unbleached white flower
⅓ cup	85 mL	shelled sunflower seeds
sunflower seeds, for garnish		

In a large bowl, dissolve the yeast in the warm water and add the honey; set aside. Add the salt and butter to the pumpkin purée; mix well and stir into the yeast. Work in 3½ cups (825 mL) of flour with a hand-held mixer or the dough-hook attachment on an electric mixer—mix for 2 minutes. If the dough is too sticky, keep adding small amounts of flour until the dough comes away from the sides of the bowl. Stir in ⅓ cup (85 mL) sunflower seeds. Let the dough rest in a warm place, covered with a damp towel, for 2 to 3 minutes. Place the dough in a clean, lightly greased bowl and turn the dough to coat it. Cover the dough with a damp towel and set in a warm place to rise until doubled in bulk. Turn the dough out, punch down, and form the dough into two small loaves. Place in lightly oiled 9-inch (23-cm) loaf pans. Brush the tops of the loaves lightly with water and sprinkle with additional sunflower seeds. Cover the loaves with a damp towel, set in a warm place, and let them rise for about 40 minutes. Bake in a pre-heated 350°F (180°C) oven for about 45 minutes or until the tops are browned. Turn out and cool on a rack.
Yield ✻ 2 loaves.

French tarragon

Artemisia dracunculus var. *sativa*

Tender perennial.
Height 60 to 120 cm; spread 30 to 45 cm.
Branching herb with smooth, shiny, dark-green, lobe-shaped leaves.

*T*arragon always signals gourmet quality to me. True French tarragon doesn't grow from seed, but must be raised painstakingly from tiny cuttings. It's a slow, laborious process to get those cuttings to sufficient size to plant into the garden. Perhaps it's because I understand the effort that goes into growing it, but for me, the presence of tarragon on the menu suggests a truly fine dining experience. ❋ Tarragon's slight anise flavour requires deft judgement in the kitchen. It may be overpowering in excess, so use a light touch.

Try it!

***Artemisia dracunculus* var. *sativa* (French tarragon, true tarragon)**
is the only variety worth growing: the flavour is distinctive, with a slight hint of anise—wonderful!

Planting

Grow from young plants purchased from a garden centre. French tarragon cannot be grown from seed.

How much✻ At least two plants.

When✻ Around the date of the last average spring frost.

Where✻ Full sun. Demands light, well-drained soil; cannot tolerate wet or poorly drained soil. Space plants at least 60 cm apart.

Give tarragon plenty of room in the garden.

Care and Nurture

Tarragon requires some care to grow well. Water regularly to keep plant lush and full. Tarragon doesn't require much fertilizer. Tarragon spreads, like mint, by underground runners, but is not nearly as invasive or hard to control. Tarragon tends to die back or get woody in the centre; it requires regular division and should be renewed every 3 or 4 years. Because tarragon is not completely hardy, it requires mulching in the fall for winter protection.

Harvesting

The leaves can be harvested from early spring until fall.

For best flavour✻ Choose tender growth; harvest only as much as you need immediately.

Leaves✻ Harvest individual leaves by clipping the leaf stalk where it attaches to the stem. Cut sprigs where they attach to the main growing stem; use whole or strip the leaves. Discard tough stalks or use on the barbecue.

Flowers✻ Edible, but not normally eaten.

Preserving the Harvest

Tarragon is best used fresh, but can be preserved by freezing. Tarragon is also commonly preserved in vinegar—tarragon vinegar is a typical gourmet product. Don't bother drying tarragon: it loses its essential oils when dried.

Tips

✻ Never buy Russian tarragon (*Artemisia dracunculus dracunculoides*)! Its flavour is poor—in fact, it's almost tasteless. If you see tarragon seed for sale, it will definitely be the inferior Russian tarragon, so don't buy it. The true French variety can only be propagated vegetatively.

✻ Tarragon prefers warm but not hot locations in full sun. I like to plant mine in a sunny location that is protected from the hot late-afternoon sun.

Excellent with Savory Mayonnaise
(see page 166).
—John

Tarragon–Lemon Crab Cakes

1 7.5-oz. can	1 213-g can	crab meat and liquid
2	2	medium eggs
¼ cup	60 mL	diced carrots
¼ cup	60 mL	diced zucchini
¼ cup	60 mL	diced onion
2 tsp.	10 mL	vegetable oil
2 tbsp.	30 mL	dried tarragon leaves
2 tbsp.	30 mL	lemon juice
2 cups	500 mL	fresh white bread crumbs (approx.)
1 tbsp.	15 mL	chopped parsley
salt and lemon pepper, to taste		
vegetable oil for frying		
1	1	lemon or lime, cut in wedges

Mix together crab meat and eggs. In a sauté pan over medium heat, cook the carrots, zucchini, and onion in oil, stirring occasionally, for 4 to 5 minutes. Cool for 5 minutes. Add the vegetables to the crab meat-egg mixture. In a small saucepan, combine the tarragon and lemon juice; reduce over medium heat until the lemon juice has been absorbed. Add the tarragon to the crabmeat mix. Add the bread crumbs slowly, mixing constantly to ensure the mixture does not become too dry. Add chopped parsley, salt, and pepper. Form the mixture into cakes. Heat the oil in a sauté pan and cook the cakes gently on one side for about 2 minutes. Turn the cakes over and cook for 1 minute. Transfer cakes onto a baking sheet and place in the oven at 400°F (200°C) for 5 minutes. Serve immediately with lemon or lime wedges.

Hint❋ The texture of the cakes should allow them to be shaped without falling apart. If cakes are too dry, add an extra egg. If cakes are too moist, add more bread crumbs.

Your scrumptious secret recipe for people who sat around your firepit too long or just piled out of their trailer hoping for breakfast!
—Joyce

Midnight Eggs with Camembert and Tarragon

10	10	large fresh eggs
⅓ cup	75 mL	cubed Camembert or brie
½ tsp.	2 mL	freshly ground black pepper
1 tbsp.	15 mL	chopped fresh tarragon
½ tsp.	2 mL	salt
½ tsp.	2 mL	good-quality curry powder
⅓ cup	75 mL	dry white wine
or		
2 tbsp.	25 mL	dry sherry
¼ cup	50 mL	butter (not margarine)

Beat eggs gently with a fork. Combine with remaining ingredients, except butter. Melt butter in a large, well-seasoned frying pan. Pour in egg mixture and cook over very low heat. Stir and fold eggs gently, almost as if you were making mini-omelettes. Do not overcook. Spoon onto heated plates and serve with fresh raspberries or a melon wedge. Toast some real New York or Montreal-style bagels and serve with a high-quality Seville marmalade—preferably the one you made in February. Do not forget to add the best crisp white wine your budget will allow! Serves 4 to 5.

Tarragon is an essential ingredient in Dijon mustard. It's also used for seafood, poultry, beef, eggs, salads, soups, quiche, and vinegars.

Mix tarragon with plain yogurt or cottage cheese to eat with salads or fresh vegetables.

181

This soup freezes well—make extra for easy meal planning.
—John

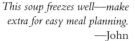

Tomato and Tarragon Soup

1 tbsp.	15 mL	vegetable oil
3 cups	750 mL	finely chopped onion
3	3	garlic cloves, crushed
5	5	large tomatoes, peeled, seeded, and chopped
1½ cups	375 mL	dry white wine
2 tbsp.	30 mL	brown sugar
1 tbsp.	15 mL	dried tarragon
2 cups	500 mL	chicken stock
salt and ground black pepper		
chopped chives or parsley, to garnish		

In a large saucepan over medium heat, stir together oil, onion, and garlic. Cook onion until lightly browned, about 10 to 12 minutes. Add the tomatoes, wine, brown sugar, tarragon, and chicken stock. Cover the saucepan, reduce heat to low, and cook for 25 to 30 minutes. Remove from the heat, add seasoning, and cool for 10 minutes. Blend the soup in a food processor into a purée. Return to the saucepan, bring to a simmer over medium heat, and check seasoning. Garnish with chopped chives or parsley and serve.

Hint ✳ To peel tomatoes: With the point of a small, sharp knife, remove the eye of each tomato. On the base of each tomato, mark an X. Don't cut too deep—just score the skin. Place the tomatoes in enough boiling water to cover them. Turn heat down to simmer and cook the tomatoes for 40 to 45 seconds. Drain the tomatoes and cool under cold water.

Serve this dish with rice—delicious!
—John

Lemon-Tarragon Chicken

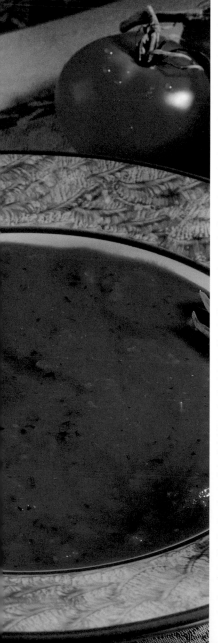

2	2	garlic cloves, minced
2 tbsp.	30 mL	white wine
1 tbsp.	15 mL	dry sherry
½ tsp.	2.5 mL	seasoned lemon pepper
1 tbsp.	15 mL	fresh tarragon leaves
or		
½ tbsp.	7.5 mL	dried tarragon
2 tbsp.	30 mL	vegetable oil
6	6	boneless, skinless chicken breasts
2 cups	500 mL	white mushrooms, quartered
1 tbsp.	15 mL	lemon juice
1	1	lemon, cut into wedges

In a medium bowl, mix garlic, white wine, sherry, lemon pepper, and tarragon. Place the chicken breast in the mixture; cover and refrigerate for one hour. In a 12-inch (30-cm) skillet, heat the oil over medium heat. Place the chicken breasts (presentation side down) in the skillet. Cook the chicken for 6 to 7 minutes or until the underside is golden-brown. Reduce heat to medium-low and turn chicken breasts over. Cook for 7 to 8 minutes or until the meat is no longer pink. Remove chicken from the pan, cover, and keep in a warm place; return pan to heat. Increase heat to medium-high and add the mushrooms; cook, stirring constantly. Add the lemon juice; cook for 1 minute. Spoon the mushrooms over the chicken; garnish with lemon wedges.
Variation Either brown mushrooms or oyster mushrooms could be used in place of white mushrooms.

183

thyme

Thymus spp.

Tender perennial; ornamental varieties are hardy.

Height 15 to 50 cm; spread 15 to 30 cm.

Herb with small, dark-green or variegated leaves with hairy undersides and tiny, tubular, lavender, mauve, pink, purple, or white flowers borne in loose whorls.

One of my favourite herbs is English thyme. I prefer its strong taste to the milder French thyme, and I find it easier to harvest. Cut a few stems and then, holding the stems over a bowl, run your thumb and index finger along them, against the leaves. The leaves will fall off easily. Discard the stems. My daughter-in-law Valerie uses thyme in two of her favourite homemade soups, roasted squash soup and onion soup, and I just love them! ❋ Thyme is the underlying flavour in countless dishes. Unlike sage or rosemary, it does not overpower food, but accompanies it subtly. Thyme flowers may be sweeter and more pungent—use them with care.

Try these!

***Thymus vulgaris* (English thyme, German thyme, winter thyme, common thyme)** ❋ Most common variety; broad-leaf variety; grows vigorously, with a full, strong flavour

***Thymus vulgaris* (French thyme, summer thyme)** ❋ Narrow-leaf variety; greyer and sweeter than English thyme

***Thymus* x *citriodorus* (lemon thyme)** ❋ Best for tea; less pungent, with a citrus flavour, and thus better used in desserts and custards

Thyme's essential oil, thymol, can be used to preserve meat. Thymol is also used as the fungicidal ingredient in mildew-control products, and serves as an important component of many mouth-washes, lozenges, cough syrups, colognes, detergents, and toothpastes.

Planting

Thyme is best grown from young plants purchased from a garden centre.

How much✳ One plant of each type you enjoy.

When✳ As soon as the ground can be worked; quite frost-tolerant.

Where✳ Full sun. Grows well in containers. Prefers light, sandy, well-drained soil; will grow in poor soil. Space plants 45 cm apart.

Care and Nurture

Thyme is easy to grow! Trim lightly after flowering to encourage compact, bushy growth. Fertilize only lightly for best leaf flavour. Thyme does not like to dry out, but overwatering and excessive fertilizer make the leaves taste bland. To ensure continued vigour in perennial varieties, divide the plants every 3 to 4 years.

golden thyme

lemon-scented thyme

Thyme grown in
and around Grasse,
in southern France,
is used in perfumeries.
The thyme also
supplies bees with
pollen, yielding the
thyme-flavoured
honey that is sold
in district markets.

Harvesting

When gathering wild thyme, taste and smell the
plants as you pick to find those that are the
most aromatic. For maximum leaf production,
don't let the plant flower.

For best flavour✻ If you're harvesting leaves,
pick them just before the plants bloom; if
you're harvesting flowers, pick them just as
they open.

Leaves✻ Harvest throughout the season, as
needed. Thyme leaves are too small to pick
individually. Clip upper stems; use whole or
strip leaves from tougher stems. Throw stems
on the barbecue to add a lovely aroma to the
smoke.

Flowers✻ Pick flowers as they appear. Flowers
grow in clusters; clip cluster from growing
stem and gently separate into individual
florets.

Preserving the Harvest

In milder climates, thyme is an evergreen, so
fresh leaves can be picked year-round. Thyme
leaves dry well and can also be preserved by
the ice-cube method (see page 26). Thyme
flowers should be used fresh.

Thyme makes an excellent rock garden plant.

Tips

* Culinary varieties will generally overwinter if you are careful about the location. Find a sheltered spot with good snow cover and light, sandy soil. In most areas of Canada, perennial thymes require mulching and protection to survive the winter.

* Although we have listed only a few common varieties, there are more than 120 varieties of thyme, some from Europe, western Asia, North Africa, and the Canary Islands. Here are some other edible varieties you may want to try.
Golden lemon thyme (*Thymus* x *citriodorus* 'Aureas') has a bright lemon flavour; its leaves have scattered yellow edges. The unique aroma of **caraway thyme (*Thymus herba-barona*)** is a cross between sweet caraway and pine. **Orange balsam thyme (*Thymus* x Orange Balsam)** has a wonderful orange fragrance and flavour. **Nutmeg thyme (*Thymus praecox* ssp. *articus*)** is a small-leaved trailing species with the scent and flavour of nutmeg. **Oregano thyme (*Thymus* sp.)** bears a hint of oregano in its scent and flavour.

* **Wild thyme (*Thymus serpyllum*)**, also known as mother of thyme or broad-leaved thyme, can be used for cooking, but makes a better groundcover. It exudes a lovely scent when stepped on. **Woolly mother of thyme** or **woolly thyme (*Thymus pseudolanuginosus*)** is another ornamental variety with a superb scent, but is not recommended for cooking. Try growing it around patio stones or in a rock garden.

One of the most important herbs in human civilization, thyme was cultivated in Sumeria as early as 3000 BC. Indeed, an ancient Sumerian stone tablet mentions thyme in what could be the world's oldest prescription: "After grinding together the seeds of saffron and thyme and putting them in beer, the patient shall drink."

*Serve with Chives Biscuits
(see page 211).*
—John

Barley–Vegetable Soup

4 10-oz. cans	4 284-mL cans	chicken or beef bouillon
2 tbsp.	30 mL	vegetable oil
1	1	large onion, finely diced
2	2	celery stalks, finely diced
1 cup	250 mL	carrot, finely diced
1½ cups	375 mL	white mushrooms, quartered
1	1	bay leaf
1 sprig	1 sprig	thyme
¾ cup	175 mL	medium pearl barley
salt and ground black pepper, to taste		
1 tbsp.	15 mL	chopped parsley
1 tbsp.	15 mL	chopped chives

In a medium saucepan, add 1 can of bouillon and 2 cups water to the barley and bring to a boil over medium heat; simmer uncovered for 1 hour, or until the liquid is absorbed. In a large saucepan over medium heat, add the oil and sauté the onion, celery, carrots, and mushrooms. Cook, stirring occasionally, for 5 minutes or until the vegetables are softened. Add the remaining bouillon, bay leaf, and thyme; bring to a boil, reduce heat, and simmer for 15 minutes. Remove the thyme stem and bay leaf. Add the barley and simmer; season to taste. Serve soup in heated bowls, garnished with chopped parsley and chives.
Variation❋ Brown or oyster mushrooms can also be used.
Hint❋ This soup freezes well.

The tantalizing flavour of
perfect roast beef enhanced
by mustard and fresh herbs.
—Joyce

Lois' Roast Beef with Herbs

5 lb.	2.5 kg	sirloin or prime-rib roast
4 tbsp.	50 mL	finely chopped or grated onion
3 tbsp.	50 mL	German mustard
1 tbsp.	15 mL	fresh black pepper
2 tbsp.	25 mL	chopped fresh savory
2 tbsp.	25 mL	chopped fresh thyme
2 tbsp.	25 mL	chopped fresh oregano

Wipe roast very dry with paper towels.
Combine onion, mustard, and pepper.
Spread mixture all over meat surface.
(If you wish, score the roast as you would
a ham before covering with seasoning and
herbs. This will enable all flavours to
penetrate more thoroughly.) Combine herbs
and work them into the onion-mustard
spread. Refrigerate on a glass or pottery
platter, tightly covered, for 18 to 24 hours.
Leave at room temperature 1 hour before
roasting. Place roast on a rack in an open
shallow pan. Roast according to doneness
chart below. Use a meat thermometer for
the perfect temperature! Cover lightly with
foil and allow to stand at room temperature
15 minutes before carving. Serves 6. Serve
with mashed potatoes, gravy, and a wide
variety of seasonal vegetables.
Hint ❋ When roasting at 325°F (160°C):
   3 hours = Rare (140°F);
   3½ hours = Medium (160°F);
   4 to 4½ hours = Well (170°F).

A rich, savoury dish.
—John

Potatoes with Cheese, Herbs, and Eggs

3 tbsp.	45 mL	melted butter
salt and ground black pepper, to taste		
6	6	large potatoes, cooked and sliced
3	3	large tomatoes, in ¼-inch (0.5-cm) slices
1 tbsp.	15 mL	chopped fresh basil
1 tbsp.	15 mL	chopped fresh chives
1 tbsp.	15 mL	chopped fresh thyme
½ lb.	225 g	grated mozzarella cheese
6	6	eggs, lightly beaten
½ cup	125 mL	grated Parmesan cheese
⅓ cup	85 mL	melted butter

Prepare a 13 x 9-inch (33 x 23-cm) baking dish by brushing it with melted butter. Sprinkle lightly with salt and pepper. Layer the sliced potatoes in the dish and season with more salt and pepper. Lay the sliced tomatoes on top of the potatoes and sprinkle with the chopped herbs. Sprinkle the grated mozzarella cheese over the dish. Pour the lightly beaten eggs on top of the dish. Sprinkle with the grated Parmesan, salt, and pepper; drizzle ⅓ cup (85 mL) melted butter over dish. Bake at 350°F (180°C) for 25 to 30 minutes, or until the eggs are cooked and the cheese is melted. (To brown the cheese, finish dish under the broiler for 2 minutes.)

Thyme should be added to recipes 10 to 15 minutes before the end of the cooking process.

*Herb Butter (see page 30) is
wonderful on the side of this dish.*
—John

Salmon with Thyme, Orange, and Lemon Pepper

4 6-oz.	4 180-g	salmon steaks
1 tbsp.	15 mL	vegetable oil
3 tsp.	15 mL	minced thyme
2 tsp.	10 mL	grated orange rind
2 tbsp.	30 mL	orange juice
salt and lemon pepper, to taste		
1	1	lemon, cut into wedges
fresh thyme sprigs for garnish		

Place the salmon in a shallow ovenproof
baking dish and coat with oil. Add the
minced thyme, orange rind, orange juice,
salt, and lemon pepper. Cover dish with
kitchen wrap and refrigerate for 1 hour.
Remove dish from refrigerator and bake
at 400°F (200°C) for 15 to 20 minutes or
until fish flakes easily with a fork. Garnish
with lemon wedges and sprigs of thyme.

For a special treat, sprinkle freshly clipped
thyme over very ripe tomatoes with a dash
of thyme oil and balsamic vinegar.

Thyme is lovely with oregano and savory.
Thyme and marjoram are complementary herbs
and are often mixed together.

lemon verbena

Aloysia triphylla [aka *A. citriodora, Lippia triphylla*]

Tender perennial; grown as an annual in most parts of Canada.
Height 1 to 2 m; spread 45 cm to 1 m.
Herb with stiff, apple-green, willowy leaves and small,
  pale-lilac flowers in pyramid-shaped clusters.

*L*emon verbena is my favourite lemon-
scented herb. I love running my fingers
along its long, smooth leaves to release
its gorgeous lemony aroma. I prefer to grow
verbena in pots, so I can move it from time to
time to take advantage of warmth and light.
❋ *Lemon verbena produces an exceptionally lovely scent and has the best
lemon flavour of any herb. The
tiny white blossoms are also
edible and delicious—
too bad verbena rarely
flowers in my area!*

Try it!

Only ***Aloysia triphylla*** (**common lemon verbena**) is readily available
  in North America.

Planting

Lemon verbena is best grown from young plants purchased from a garden centre.

How much❋ At least two plants.

When❋ One to two weeks after the date of the last average spring frost in your area.

Where❋ Full sun, sheltered; a south-facing wall is ideal. Prefers rich, well-drained soil. Space plants at least 30 cm apart.

Care and Nurture

Lemon verbena is easy to grow! It loves heat, but don't let it dry out.

Harvesting

Harvest leaves throughout the growing season. The flowers are also edible and tasty, but verbena rarely blooms in Canada's short growing season.

For best flavour❋ Harvest mature plants: the lemon fragrance and flavour grow stronger with age.

Leaves❋ Strip leaves from the woody stems with your fingers; discard any tough stalks.

Flowers❋ Harvest as they appear; clip from stem and use whole.

Preserving the Harvest

Lemon verbena leaves will retain their flavour for years. Dry and place immediately in an airtight jar, and keep the jar in a cool, dark place. You can also freeze the chopped leaves and flowers; use the ice-cube method (see page 26).

Tips

❋ Give lemon verbena the sunniest location you can. The plants respond well to warmth and light.

❋ Lemon verbena usually grows best when it is free of competition. However, I like to plant lemon verbena in a pot with 'Dark Opal' basil: the plants' contrasting leaf colours look fantastic together, they like the same growing conditions, and one never overgrows the other.

Fresh Fruit Salad with Lemon Verbena

In summer, the small white flowers of lemon verbena have a wonderful citrus fragrance; use sprigs with flowers attached as a garnish.
—John

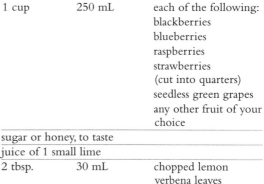

1 cup	250 mL	each of the following:
		blackberries
		blueberries
		raspberries
		strawberries
		(cut into quarters)
		seedless green grapes
		any other fruit of your choice
sugar or honey, to taste		
juice of 1 small lime		
2 tbsp.	30 mL	chopped lemon verbena leaves

Gently rinse the berries and dry any excess moisture. Mix the berries and add the grapes. Add sugar or honey to taste. Pour lime juice over the fruit. Add chopped lemon verbena leaves. Gently mix the berries, being careful not to bruise the fruit. Marinate for 1 hour, then serve.

Hint✷ General notes on fruit salads: Soft fruits such as bananas, kiwis, watermelon, and ripe papaya should be added to the salad at the last moment. Watermelon and other melons make glazes and marinades watery. The addition of a peeled, diced green apple gives a great contrast of texture and flavour. Blanch lemon, lime, or orange zest for 30 seconds in boiling water, rinse under cold water, and add to fruit salads for extra texture and flavour.

Hint✷ Marinades, dressings, and syrups: Simple marinades made from lemon or lime juice with a small amount of honey or sugar make a light syrup for any fruit salad. If you are using canned fruits (e.g., pineapple chunks, mandarin orange segments, pears peaches, apricots, etc.), reduce the fruit liquid by half with a cinnamon stick and a clove to make an excellent marinade. Cool the syrup before pouring over fruit. Use low-fat flavoured yogourt with a squeeze of fresh lime juice and a spoonful of ground cinnamon to make an excellent fruit salad dressing or fresh fruit dip.

You can replace the lemon verbena leaves with mint leaves for a refreshing change.
—John

Honeydew Granita

⅓ cup	85 mL	water
3 tbsp.	45 mL	granulated sugar
2 tsp.	10 mL	finely grated lemon rind
2	2	fresh lemon verbena leaves, finely chopped
3 to 4 cups	750 to 1000 mL	honeydew melon, peeled, cubed, and seeds removed (1 small)
3 tbsp.	45 mL	lime juice

Toss a few lemon verbena blooms into a bowl of fresh raspberries or strawberries.

In a medium saucepan, mix the sugar, water, and lemon rind. Bring to a boil over medium-high heat; stir until the sugar is dissolved. Reduce heat to medium-low and simmer the syrup for 5 minutes. Remove from heat; add the chopped lemon verbena. In a food processor with a steel blade, purée the cubed melon. In a large bowl, mix the purée and the cooled syrup; add lime juice to taste. Put the mixture into a shallow tray or freezer trays. Freeze the mixture until it is firm but not frozen solid. Re-mix the granita by hand or in the food processor. Freeze the mixture again for 2 to 3 hours, until it is quite firm. Remove from freezer. When the granita is soft enough to serve, scoop into chilled glasses.

A fast and delicious pie made with backyard apples and the light essence of lemon verbena.
—Joyce

Farmhouse Apple Pie with Lemon Verbena

Add chopped lemon verbena to a low-fat yogourt to make a tasty fruit-salad dressing or fruit dip. Finely chopped lemon verbena leaves mixed with honey and lemon juice make excellent syrup for serving with fresh berries.

Flaky pastry for 2 crust pie:

2 cups	500 mL	flour
⅔ cups	150 mL	shortening
½ tsp.	2 mL	salt
2 tbsp.	25 mL	sugar
3 tbsp.	50 mL	ground almonds (optional)
1 tsp.	5 mL	pure vanilla extract
3 to 5 tbsp.	45 to 60 mL	water
6		large tart cooking apples
¼ cup	50 mL	flour
⅔ to ¾ cup	150 to 175 mL	sugar
¼ cup	50 mL	honey
½ tsp.	2 mL	nutmeg
1 tsp.	5 mL	cinnamon
1 tsp.	5 mL	finely chopped lemon verbena
milk or cream and sugar for top glaze		

Prepare pastry by the usual method and chill. The addition of sugar, almonds, and vanilla gives a great flavour and texture. Combine the apples (peel if you wish) with the remaining ingredients and stir thoroughly until the juices and sugar form a nice syrup. To make an old-fashioned rustic pie, roll the pastry into a large circle and transfer to a cookie sheet. Spoon the apple filling into the centre of the pastry. Carefully bring the edges of the pie dough towards the centre, leaving some of the filling exposed. Crimp some of the overlapping folds together to form the rustic appearance. Brush the pastry with milk or cream and dust lightly with sugar. Bake at 425°F (220°C) for 15 minutes; reduce the temperature to 350°F (175°C) and bake for approximately 35 to 40 minutes or until the apples test done and pie is golden-brown. Serve warm with brown sugar and vanilla-flavoured whipping cream for something very special.

For the Adventurous...

This section discusses 75 other herbs and edible flowers that you might want to try to expand your interest in culinary herbs. Some of these species may not be widely available, may require special care, or may be restricted in some jurisdictions; check with your local garden centre for information appropriate to your region. The species are listed in alphabetical order of their Latin names, because common names can vary from place to place.

All the species discussed here are edible, but as always, we recommend you err on the side of caution. Never eat any herb or flower unless you are certain you have identified it correctly, and do not eat the herb in large quantities until you know you are not sensitive to it. Wash all herbs and flowers thoroughly before eating them, and do not eat herbs or flowers that have been exposed to unknown pesticides or picked from uncontrolled locations (such as roadsides or ditches). Whenever possible, eat only plants you have grown yourself.

You can find further cultivation information for many of the species discussed here in the books *Lois Hole's Bedding Plant Favorites* (1994) and *Lois Hole's Perennial Favorites* (1995).

yarrow
Achillea millefolium

Hardy perennial

Height 30–90 cm; spread to 60 cm

Strongly aromatic, feathery, fern-like leaves and clusters of tiny white flowers.

IN THE KITCHEN * The young leaves (with stalks removed) can be used in salads. The flowers can be sprinkled over salads and make a lovely, delicate garnish for any dish. Both the leaves and flowers should be eaten in moderation, however.

yarrow

PLANT NOTES * The genus names of species refers to the mythical Achilles, who is said to have used yarrow to heal his men's wounds. * **Similar species:** The leaves of English mace (*Achillea ageratum*) can be stuffed into chicken or added to salads, rice and pasta dishes, soups, and stews.

goutweed

Aegopodium podograria

Very hardy perennial

Height 30–90 cm; spread indefinite

Long-stalked leaves and tiny white flowers on umbels.

IN THE KITCHEN * Goutweed tastes like spinach. Young leaves may be used in salads and soups or as a vegetable.

PLANT NOTES * Goutweed is an aggressive, invasive species and must be contained or it will take over the garden. * During the medieval era, goutweed was cultivated in British monasteries.

giant hyssop

(anise hyssop)

Agastache foeniculum

Perennial

Height 60–150 cm; spread to 45 cm

In summer, giant hyssop sports purple flower spikes, 8 to 10 mm long.

IN THE KITCHEN * Use the aniseed-flavoured leaves in green salads, fruit salads, fruit tarts, and pea- or lamb-based dishes. The leaves are also good for teas. The flowers are also edible, with an anise flavour and a light honey scent.

PLANT NOTES * *Similar species:* Korean mint (*Agastache rugosa*) and Mexican agastache (*Agastache mexicana*) can be used like giant hyssop. Both have a flavour reminiscent of mint and aniseed. The seed heads also look wonderful in dried floral arrangements. * Giant hyssop attracts bees. The plant was used by beekeepers of the late 19th century to produce honey with a slight aniseed flavour. * Giant hyssop flowers were often included in Cree medicine bundles.

hollyhocks

Alcea rosea

Annual

Height 1.2–1.5 m; spread 35–60 cm

Large, crinkly, dark-green leaves and large (10 cm), single flowers atop strong, tall stems.

IN THE KITCHEN * The flowers are excellent crystallized and can be used to accent puddings, fools, fruit salads, and green salads. They also add a nice flavour to soups.

PLANT NOTES * Hollyhocks bloom all summer and make an gorgeous accent plant in rows against fences or walls. They also look great in cottage gardens and perennial beds. * Never plant hollyhocks near mint: hollyhocks are prone to rust and may spread it to mint.

garlic

garlic
Allium spp.

Perennial; most gardeners treat as an annual

Height 15–20 cm; spread 20–30 cm

Easily recognized by its white, papery-skinned bulbs, tall, hollow leaves, and globular flower clusters.

IN THE KITCHEN ✳ Garlic, one of the most popular culinary herbs in the world, adds delightful flavour to soups, spreads, meats, bread, pickles, Caesar salad, escargot, and much, much more. To add subtle garlic flavour, rub your utensils with a clove before the meal.

PLANT NOTES ✳ In the garden, interplantings of garlic are said to repel insects and other pests. ✳ Braided garlic makes an intriguing rustic decoration. ✳ In ancient Egypt, a slave could be purchased in exchange for 7 kg of garlic.

angelica
Angelica archangelica

Short-lived perennial or biennial

Height 1–2.5 m; spread 0.5–1 m

Thick, hollow stems, long-stalked, deeply divided leaves, and umbels of very small green-white flowers.

IN THE KITCHEN ✳ Angelica's small flowers, which should be picked as they open in the spring, taste as good as they smell. They are excellent in fruit salads, green salads, and cream cheese. Angelica stems may be eaten as a vegetable; they can also be candied. Angelica may be used as flavouring for rhubarb, in orange marmalade, and in citrus sorbets.

angelica

PLANT NOTES ✳ Angelica is an ingredient in liqueurs and aperitifs like Benedictine. ✳ Angelica looks wonderful in the garden. Bees are attracted to it, too. ✳ Crushed angelica leaves freshen the air. ✳ Angelica was believed to protect against evil and cure all ills—an angelic herb indeed.

chervil
(curled chervil)
Anthriscus cerefolium

Annual

Height 30–60 cm; spread to 70 cm

Chervil has hollow, furrowed stems, divided leaves, and white flowers.

IN THE KITCHEN * Chervil's calcium-rich, subtly flavoured leaves are often added to potatoes, spring soups, salads, eggs, and fish, especially in French cuisine. It is an essential ingredient in ravigote sauces. Chervil is often substituted for tarragon or parsley, and makes an attractive garnish. The leaves should be cut before the plant flowers; use fresh.

chervil

PLANT NOTES * Chervil was cultivated by ancient Syrians, who ate it raw or boiled. * According to folklore, chervil makes one merry, prods the memory, and gives the aged a surge of youthful vigour.

Easy Ways to Use Herbs and Edible Flowers Every Day

* Add chopped fresh herbs to a tomato, cheese, and onion sandwich.

* Garnish vichyssoise with violets or chive blossoms; add long "sticks" of chives. Garnish chilled summer soups with nasturtiums or chive blossoms.

* Broil a quick bruschetta with mixed fresh herbs, balsamic vinegar, and very ripe Roma tomatoes.

* Soften high-quality vanilla ice cream, add fuchsia, pansy, dianthus, or borage petals, and refreeze. Place a careful scoop on a cantaloupe or in stem glasses. Garnish with a matching flower.

* Add chopped fresh or dried herbs to your favorite dumpling recipe for stew or thick vegetable soup.

* Popcorn becomes special when you add finely chopped herbs and lots of black pepper to the melted butter before tossing.

* For a different flavour allow some chopped lemon grass and Vietnamese cilantro to cool and steep overnight in hot crabapple juice. Strain and prepare jelly as usual.

* Combine cooked new potatoes and green beans with butter, lemon juice, and chopped marjoram, rosemary, and thyme.

* Brush a sliced bagel with oil and sprinkle with chopped basil, oregano, and thyme. Top with Parmesan or mozzarella cheese and broil.

* Herb jelly may be made from your favorite recipe for mint jelly. Use your favourite herb or combination of herbs in place of mint.

snapdragons

snapdragons

Antirrhinum majus

Annual

Height 15–90 cm; spread 25–30 cm

Brightly coloured, distinctive snap-jawed flowers blooming along tall, often fuzzy flower spikes.

IN THE KITCHEN * Sprinkle snapdragons on green salads and fruit salads, or use them as an edible garnish. Be cautious—some varieties are more bitter than others.

PLANT NOTES * Snapdragons have excellent frost tolerance and can be planted as soon as the ground is workable. * Snapdragons come in many colours—red, bronze, lavender, pink, yellow, orange, and white—with new shades appearing every year. Use them for borders, window boxes, backgrounds, container plantings, and feature plants.

horseradish

Armoracia rusticana

Very hardy perennial

Height 30–120 cm; spread 60–90 cm

Horseradish has long, ovate leaves and a thick, branched taproot.

IN THE KITCHEN * The young, fresh leaves are quite mild, and excellent in salads or sandwiches. The grated fleshy root of the horseradish is a popular accompaniment to roast beef, chicken, and hard-boiled eggs.

PLANT NOTES * Horseradish's potent flavour can be weakened if it gets too much water and fertilizer—it's one plant that actually benefits from neglect! * Horseradish roots can reach to 60 cm deep. * The research centre in Brooks, Alberta once grew horseradish to study as an export crop. When the trial was complete, it was extremely difficult to get rid of the plant, regardless of the treatments they tried, ranging from tilling to herbicides. Once you grow horseradish, you'll have it forever!

wild horseradish

red orach

(mountain spinach)

Atriplex hortensis 'Rubra'

Annual

Height to 1.2 m; spread to 30 cm

An upright plant with purple-red triangular leaves and purple-red stems; gold and purple varieties are also available.

IN THE KITCHEN * Young leaves make a colourful and tasty addition to salads. Old leaves may be steamed like spinach. The leaves may also be used in soups, game meat dishes, and breads.

PLANT NOTES * Red orach looks great planted in a container.

red orach

Fresh Basil Pesto

Serve this pesto with minestrone soup, stirred into freshly cooked pasta, on toast as a spread, or with polenta.
—John

4 cups	1 L	basil leaves, packed
8	8	garlic cloves
2 cups	500 mL	pine nuts
1½ cup	375 mL	grated Romano *or* Parmesan cheese
1¾ cup	440 mL	olive oil
ground black pepper		
¼ cup	65 mL	warm water (approx.)

In a food processor, process basil leaves, black pepper, and garlic into a fine paste. Add pine nuts and grated cheese; blend to a purée. With the machine running, add the oil in a steady stream; process until the mixture is smooth and creamy. The mixture should resemble a smooth paste after the oil has been added. If the mixture is too thick, add some warm water with the machine running.

Variation* To make sorrel pesto, use 4 cups (1 L) sorrel and ⅔ cup (150 mL) fresh parsley in place of the basil.

Hint* The choice of fresh versus dried (commercially prepared) Parmesan is a matter of cost, quality, taste, and convenience. Prepared Parmesan bears little resemblance to the real thing, but it will work in this recipe. Keep a piece of fresh Parmesan in the fridge, or grate fresh Parmesan and keep it in the freezer in sealed plastic bags.

Hint* You can make pesto in bulk and freeze for use in the winter. Make the base with basil leaves and olive oil: mix the basil and oil in a processor into a thick paste. Don't add the cheese or nuts. Store the paste in the refrigerator and add the other ingredients later, as needed. The paste will keep for 3 months in the refrigerator.

upland cress

(winter cress)

Barbarea verna

Annual

Height 30–90 cm

An upright-growing plant, upland cress has divided lance-shaped leaves and tiny flowers.

IN THE KITCHEN * Upland cress tastes like garden cress; peppery, but more bitter than watercress. The young, tender leaves and shoots are used in salads, as a seasoning, or for garnishes. The flower buds may be used in salads and vegetable dishes. The seedlings make tasty sprouts.

tuberous begonia

Begonia x *tuberhybrida*

Annual

Height 20–30 cm; spread indefinite

A bushy, mounding annual with fuzzy, dark green leaves and large, silky, bright blooms in a wide range of colours.

IN THE KITCHEN * The young petals of tuberous begonia may be added to salads, desserts, or fish dishes.

PLANT NOTES * Eat only the petals of tuberous begonia; don't confuse them with other begonia varieties.

black mustard

Brassica nigra

Annual

Height 90–300 cm; spread 90–120 cm

Black mustard's stems are tall and many-branched, with narrow, oval leaves and bright-yellow flowers. The seeds are very dark brown.

IN THE KITCHEN * The young leaves and flowers of black mustard add a pungent dash of flavour to salads. Seeds may be used whole in curries or pickling, or ground to make mustard.

white mustard

Brassica sinapsis alba
(aka *Sinapsis alba*)

Annual

Height 20–60 cm; spread to 30 cm

Mustard features small, 4-petalled, yellow flowers atop long stems; the leaves are lobed and slightly bristly.

IN THE KITCHEN * Mustard greens make a piquant summer salad and may also be used as a pot-herb. The blossoms can be added to salads. The powdered seed, in combination with other ingredients, is used to make the popular condiment.

PLANT NOTES * Use mustard blossoms with care: they can be bitter. * Historically, mustard seed was simply pulverized and sprinkled over food. * Both Charlemagne and Shakespeare are said to have grown mustard.

capers

Capparis spinosa inermis

Tender perennial

Height to 1 m; spread to 1.5 m

A slow-growing, straggly shrub,
caper is easily recognized by its
dark-green ovate leaves and its
white to pink, 4-petalled flowers
with long pink stamens.

IN THE KITCHEN ❋ Pickled or
salted flower buds are used in
caper sauce for lamb, fish, and
hors d'oeuvres. Capers have a
natural affinity for garlic and
lemon—hence their presence
in Caesar salad. Capers are also
used in French mayonnaise-based
sauces, vinaigrettes, flavoured
butters, and tartar sauce.

peppers

Capsicum spp.

Annual

Height 30–90 cm; spread 30–90 cm

Pepper plants are typically bushy,
with thick central stalks. Depending on species, they produce
mild-flavoured bell-shaped
peppers (called "sweet" peppers)
or long, finger-shaped hot
peppers. Pepper fruits come in
many colours: orange, yellow,
green, red, and
even purple.

IN THE KITCHEN ❋ Peppers are
great in all kinds of meat dishes,
stir-fries, salads, sandwiches, and
appetizers. They can be stuffed
and pickled, too.

Cheese and Marjoram Stuffed Onions

*Excellent with broiled fish,
sautéed zucchini with cherry
tomatoes, and multi-grain rolls.*
—Joyce

4	4	medium cooking onions, peeled
oil		
dry sherry		
salt and lemon pepper, to taste		
4 tbsp.	50 mL	crushed saltines
4 tbsp.	50 mL	grated old cheddar cheese
1 tbsp.	15 mL	chopped fresh marjoram
1 tsp.	5 mL	chopped fresh thyme
1 tbsp.	15 mL	chopped fresh parsley
¼ tsp.	1 mL	dry mustard
dash	dash	Worcester-shire sauce
grated cheese		
chopped fresh parsley		

Cut the top third off each onion.
With a sharp knife, scoop out the
centre of the onions, leaving a very
thick shell. Brush the inside of each
onion lightly with oil and sherry;
sprinkle each onion with salt and
lemon pepper. Combine cracker
crumbs, 4 tbsp. (50 mL) grated
cheese, marjoram, thyme, parsley,
mustard, and Worcestershire sauce.
Spoon mixture into onions. Top with
additional grated cheese and parsley.
Bake covered at 350°F (175°C) for
30 minutes, then uncover and bake
another 15 minutes. Serves 4.

lady's smock

(cuckoo flower, bitter cress)

Cardamine pratensis

Perennial

Height 15–60 cm; spread to 30 cm

A slender plant with clusters of evenly spaced leaves on long stems and small, 4-petalled, lilac to white flowers; tends to grow in clumps.

IN THE KITCHEN ❋ The watercress-like leaves of lady's smock may be added to soups and salads or cooked as a vegetable.

PLANT NOTES ❋ Lady's smock makes a charming ornamental plant.

caraway

Carum carvi

Annual or biennial

Height to 60 cm; spread 15–30 cm

Caraway bears finely divided, fern-like leaves and dozens of tiny flowers.

IN THE KITCHEN ❋ Caraway's spicy seeds are wonderful in cabbage dishes, coleslaw, and sauerkraut; they're also good in rye bread, cakes, buns, soups, and stews. The carrot-like roots may be eaten as a vegetable; harvest them at the end of the first summer. The young leaves are tasty in salads.

PLANT NOTES ❋ Caraway is an important ingredient in liqueurs like Kummel. ❋ Caraway oil is very volatile, so never use hot, dry air to cure the seeds. ❋ According to folklore, caraway keeps lovers true to each other and cures hysteria.

bachelor's button

bachelor's button

(knapweed, chicory)

Centaurea cyanus

Annual

Height 30–90 cm; spread 15–30 cm

Tall shoots with a base of lance-shaped green leaves, topped with button-shaped flowers.

IN THE KITCHEN ❋ The little florets add wonderful colour to salads.

PLANT NOTES ❋ Bachelor's buttons, available in many colours, look great in mixed beds, meadow gardens, and backgrounds. Dried flowers can be used in potpourri, and the taller varieties make excellent cut-flowers. ❋ The genus name is derived from the legendary centaur Chiron. Chiron was known for his herb knowledge, and tradition has it that he was the first to reveal the healing properties of knapweed.

chamomile

Chamaemelum nobile

Perennial

Height to 15 cm; spread to 45 cm

Aromatic plant with finely divided foliage and apple-scented, white, daisy-like flowers.

IN THE KITCHEN ✳ Chamomile tea is commonly consumed after large meals to aid digestion. Chamomile is also used in fruit dishes and cream or light cheeses. The flowers should be cut just as they begin to droop. Dry quickly and store in dark, tightly sealed containers.

PLANT NOTES ✳ Don't confuse this species with German chamomile (*Matricaria recutita*), which is not palatable. ✳ Chamomile is a traditional groundcover of English gardens, and looks good in rock gardens or bordering lawns. It's also used to make facial oils, floral water, and compresses.

chamomile

Tarragon Cream Pesto

A great alternative to the traditional basil-based pesto.
—John

1 cup	250 mL	fresh tarragon leaves, packed
4	4	garlic cloves
salt and ground black pepper, to taste		
1 tbsp.	15 mL	drained green *or* pink peppercorns
½ cup	125 mL	fresh white bread crumbs
1 tbsp.	15 mL	lemon juice
1 cup	250 mL	pine nuts or walnuts
¼ cup	60 mL	warm water (approx.)

In a food processor, combine tarragon, garlic, salt, and pepper; blend into a fine purée. Add the peppercorns and bread crumbs; blend to a smooth paste. Add lemon juice and pine nuts or walnuts; mix until smooth. Add the oil in a steady stream with the machine running. If the purée is too thick, add a little warm water. Store pesto in a sealed jar; cover the surface with a layer of oil (this will protect it from direct exposure to the air). The oil will pick up the flavour of the pesto and can be stirred into the mixture with no problem. Refrigerate.

lamb's quarters

(fat hen)

Chenopodium album

Annual; self-sows readily

Height 60–100 cm; spread indefinite

Lamb's quarters has small, green-white flowers and green lance-shaped leaves.

IN THE KITCHEN ✳ Lamb's quarters can be cooked as a vegetable or tossed raw into salads. It contains twice as much vitamins A and C as spinach does, and was often eaten by native Americans.

PLANT NOTES ✳ Lamb's quarters is a widespread weed in western Canada—a single plant can produce up to 70,000 seeds, and each seed can remain dormant in the soil for years. If not carefully kept in its own space in the garden, this species becomes quite a nuisance.

epazote

(Mexican tea)

Chenopodium ambrosioides

Annual

Height 1.2 m; spread 75 cm

Upright plant with medium-sized, serrated, lance-shaped leaves and tiny green flowers in panicles.

IN THE KITCHEN ✳ Epazote's leaves flavour corn, bean, fish, and shellfish dishes; it is commonly used in Mexican cuisine. Eat epazote only in moderate quantities.

PLANT NOTES ✳ Epazote has a unusual scent, which many people find pleasant.

chrysanthemum

Chrysanthemum coronarium

Perennial

Height 45–60 cm; spread 40–60 cm

IN THE KITCHEN ✳ Use for teas and salads or with lamb. Chrysanthemum is excellent in soups, sauces, poultry, seafood, baked products and with spices, chocolate, orange, and lemon. The petals also make a nice garnish. Pickle the flower heads in vinegar, or blanch them and serve with soya-seasoned tofu. Chrysanthemum flowers can also be served deep-fried in a light tempura batter.

PLANT NOTES ✳ Chrysanthemums may have a fairly strong taste, depending on the variety, so use sparingly. (In China, chrysanthemum flowers are steamed and dried to make them less bitter.) Remove the base of petals before use; the bases are bitter and shouldn't be consumed. ✳ Chrysanthemums look great in containers, perennial borders, and rock gardens. ✳ Chrysanthemums are excellent cut-flowers; cut just as the flowers open and they will last for about 2 weeks in a vase. ✳ The insecticide pyrethrum is produced from a species of chrysanthemum, *Chrysanthemum cinerariaefolium*.

Edible-Flower Ice Bowls

Fantastic to look at and easy to make! A pretty bowl to serve a frozen dessert at a summer party. At Christmastime, use cranberries, holly and snips of branches off the Christmas tree instead of flowers.
—Joyce

Take 2 freezer-proof glass bowls, one about 1½ inches (4 cm) smaller in diameter than the other. Pour cold water and crushed ice into the large bowl and float the other one inside it. Fix with tape so that the rims are level, then fill the gap with ice water. Slide a colourful selection of edible flowers and leaves into the water-filled gap. Freeze overnight. Remove the bowls from the freezer and detach tape. Pour warm water into the small bowl, then lift it out. Dip the larger bowl quickly in hot water and carefully tip out the ice bowl. Place the ice bowl on plastic or a foil-lined tray and return to the freezer. When surface has refrozen, cover tightly with plastic wrap. The bowl may be prepared up to 3 weeks in advance. Place on a platter or tray covered with leaves and flowers.

Some uses for ice bowls

Serve scoops of lemon, lime and orange sherbet with strawberries and kiwi; serve scoops of vanilla ice cream and raspberry sherbet with fresh garden raspberries, with raspberry or chocolate sauce on the side; prepare a chocolate or orange mousse for the "inside" bowl and slip it back into the ice bowl and garnish with whipped cream and edible flowers.
Hint * Use distilled or boiled water for a crystal-clear ice bowl.

chrysanthemum

chicory

Cichorium intybus

Perennial

Height 30–150 cm; spread 15–45 cm

Chicory has branching stalks, oblong, toothed leaves, and clusters of blue, dandelion-like flowers.

IN THE KITCHEN * Leaves may be boiled and added to white or cheese sauces or used raw in salads. They may also be cooked and served as a vegetable. The roasted root may be used as a coffee substitute.

lemon citrus

Citrus limon

Very tender perennial; dwarf form normally grown as a houseplant in cool climates

Height 2–7 m; spread to 1 m when grown indoors

Small flowering tree forms an umbrella-like canopy of light-green, ovate leaves with pointed tips.

IN THE KITCHEN ✻ The citrus flower is very versatile. Pick flowers as they open for use in salads, stir-fries, and desserts. (Remove the green parts of the flower before eating.) The young leaves are also edible.

PLANT NOTES ✻ Similar species: orange citrus (*Citrus sinensis*) can be used in the same ways as lemon citrus, but its flavour is milder and sweeter. ✻ When grown as house-plants, lemon and orange citrus will produce only small fruits. The fruits are still edible, however, and can be used in lemonade and other drinks, desserts, salad dressings, marmalade, pickles, and meat dishes.

samphire

(sea fennel, Peter's grass, rock samphire)

Crithmum maritimum

Tender perennial

Height 15–30 cm; spread 15–30 cm

Samphire bears linear, lance-shaped leaves with a waxy coating and tiny yellow-green flowers in umbels.

IN THE KITCHEN ✻ A strongly flavoured herb, samphire may be used for pickling, salads, and herbed butters. The leaves may also be steamed in salt.

PLANT NOTES ✻ Samphire grows naturally along European coast-lines.

mitsuba

(Japanese parsley)

Cryptotaenia japonica

Perennial

Height 20–120 cm; spread 30–50 cm

Upright plant bearing trifoliate leaves with toothed leaflets.

IN THE KITCHEN ✻ Mitsuba tastes like a blend of parsley, celery, and angelica, and all parts of the herb are edible. The raw leaves and leaf stalks are used in salads and sandwiches; they may also be boiled or fried and added to soups, eggs, tempura, and fried foods. Mitsuba also makes an attractive garnish.

PLANT NOTES ✻ Unlike most herbs, this plant prefers partial shade and likes lots of water.

squash blossoms

squash blossom

Cucurbita pepo spp.

Annual

Long, thick vines bear very large, bristly leaves and bright-yellow flowers up to 10 cm deep.

IN THE KITCHEN ❋ Harvest flowers just as they are opening. They're great for stuffing (zucchini flowers are the most often used). Add squash blossoms to a salad of mixed greens, toasted walnuts, and blue cheese. They may also be battered and fried.

PLANT NOTES ❋ If you want fruit to develop on your squash plants, pick only the male flowers, found on the long, slender stems. The female flowers develop on the shorter stems. You can also tell if a flower is female by looking behind the flower: if a tiny squash fruit is developing, the flower you are looking at is female. If I know I'm going to wind up with more squash then I can possibly use, I harvest both male and female flowers.

❋ Squash makes a nice ornamental plant: many of the fat gourds are quite colourful and attractive. As a border or in large containers, the winding vines of squash contribute earthy, functional beauty to the garden. ❋ Squash blossoms are high in vitamins A and C and also contain significant amounts of iron and calcium.

Chives Biscuits

Serve with a hearty stew or soup for a satisfying winter supper, or with a green salad for a light summer meal.
—John

2 cups	500 mL	all-purpose flour
1 tbsp.	15 mL	sugar
3 tbsp.	45 mL	chopped chives
1 tbsp.	15 mL	baking powder
1 tsp.	5 mL	salt
1 cup	250 mL	margarine, cold
1½ cups	375 mL	milk
1	1	egg
2 tbsp.	30 mL	milk

In a large bowl, mix the flour, sugar, chives, baking powder, and salt. Cut the margarine into ½-inch (1-cm) pieces and add to the flour mixture. Don't overmix—the mixture should be quite coarse. Stir in the milk until the mixture begins to hold together. On a floured surface, knead the dough gently until it forms a ball. Don't overwork the dough. Roll out the dough 1 inch (2.5 cm) thick. Cut the biscuits with a 3-inch (7.5-cm) cutter and place on a baking sheet. (Dip cutter in flour if it sticks to dough.) In a small bowl, combine the egg with 2 tbsp. (30 mL) of milk. Brush the tops of the biscuits with the egg-milk mixture. Bake biscuits at 350°F (160°C) until golden-brown, about 20 to 25 minutes.
Note❋ The cutter should be pressed down firmly and not twisted. If you twist the cutter, it tends to deform the edge of the biscuits, preventing them from rising evenly.

cumin

Cuminum cyminum

Annual

Height 15–30 cm; spread 8–10 cm

Dark-green leaves divided into linear segments and umbels of tiny white or pink flowers.

IN THE KITCHEN * Cumin's flavour resembles caraway's, but it is hotter and more bitter. The seeds are roasted and added to lamb, soups, cakes, breads, cucumber, yogurt, rice, bread, devilled eggs, and potatoes. It is used in couscous, curries, pickling, and liqueurs.

PLANT NOTES * During the Middle Ages, cumin was believed to keep lovers from growing fickle and prevent poultry from running away.

dianthus

Dianthus carophyllus

Annual

Height 10–25 cm

Dianthus plants have dark-green, lance-shaped leaves and brightly coloured flowers (white, pink, crimson, and cerise) with fringed petals.

IN THE KITCHEN * Dianthus has a sweet clove flavour and may be used in syrups, vinegars, butters, cordials, marmalade, puddings, fruit pies, fruit salads, cakes, jellies, jams, and tea. The fresh flowers comple-ment salads nicely. Use only the petals, and remove the bitter heel of the petals before use.

PLANT NOTES * I recommend dianthus for borders, containers, mass plantings, rock gardens, cottage gardens, and edgings. They smell lovely, especially in the evening. The dried flowers can be used in potpourris. * All species of dianthus are edible.

dianthus

cardamom

Elettarra cardamomum

Tender perennial

Height to 3 m; spread indefinite

Cardamom has very long (60 cm), lance-shaped leaves.

IN THE KITCHEN * The aromatic seeds of cardamom are used to flavour baked items, pickles, Persian coffee, mulled wine, and fruit compotes. It is used to make ginger-bread in Germany and pastries in Scandinavia. Add ground seeds to orange marmalade, ⅛ tsp. (0.5 mL) per pint. Cardamom features significantly in Indian cuisine and is included in all the best curries; it is an especially important ingredient in the Indian spice-mixture garam masala.

PLANT NOTES ✳ Cardamom makes a good houseplant (although you may have trouble getting it to flower indoors) and grows well in the shade. ✳ Cardamom seeds are excellent in potpourris and sachets.

Vietnamese balm

Elsholtzia ciliata

Annual

Height 30–60 cm

An erect annual with oval, pointed, serrated leaves and spikes of light purple flowers.

IN THE KITCHEN ✳ Vietnamese balm resembles lemon balm in taste, and may be added raw to salads, cooked as a vegetable, made into tea, or used in fish dishes.

roquette

(arugula)

Eruca vesicaria ssp. *sativa*

Annual

Height 60–100 cm; spread 15–20 cm

An upright plant with toothed leaves and white, 4-petalled, purple-veined flowers.

IN THE KITCHEN ✳ Often included in mesclun (salad greens) mixes, rocket may also be used in stir-fries and pasta sauces. The flowers, seeds, and oil are all edible.

PLANT NOTES ✳ Roquette is best used young: the leaves may become bitter as the plant matures and flowers.

Heaven Scent Herb Pillow

Try this mixture with grapefruit mint, pineapple mint, lime mint, or spearmint!
—Joyce

½ cup	125 mL	dried lemon verbena
½ cup	125 mL	dried lavender
½ cup	125 mL	dried mint
½ cup	125 mL	dried lemon or nutmeg thyme
1½ cup	375 mL	dried rose- or lemon-scented geranium leaves
2 tbsp.	25 mL	dried rosemary

Combine ingredients thoroughly in a plastic bag. Spoon into small cotton bags, and secure with elastic bands. Put in your pillow or in an open dish by your bed and you will be lulled to sleep by the combined scents of a country flower garden!

meadowsweet

(queen of the meadow)

Filipendula ulmaria

Perennial

Height 60–120 cm; spread to 45 cm

Distinguished by 3-lobed, serrated leaves and large, fluffy heads of creamy white flowers.

IN THE KITCHEN * Flowers may be used fresh in salads or infused into oils, jams, stewed fruit, vinegars, and jellies. They may also be made into wine.

fuchsia

fuchsia

Fuchsia x *hybrida*

Annual

Height 30–60 cm; spread 15–20 cm

Extremely showy, continuously blooming plant bearing brilliantly coloured flowers.

IN THE KITCHEN * Fuchsias can be used to provide decoration for desserts. They add colour to fruit salad and beverages, too. Freeze flowers whole in individual ice cubes to add to iced tea or special cocktails. The flowers look beautiful when crystallized, but the flavour is somewhat dull. Fill individual bowls with chopped fuchsia petals, fruit salad, and frozen yogurt. Garnish with a whole fuchsia.

PLANT NOTES * Fuchsias are absolutely stunning in hanging baskets, windowboxes, and patio planters. * Fuchsias can be brought indoors in the fall, where they may continue to bloom for a short time. After the last harvest, you can trim the plants back and store them over the winter.

curry

Helichrysum italicum

Tender perennial

Height to 60 cm; spread to 1 m

A dense evergreen shrub with silver-grey leaves and clusters of yellow, button-like flowers.

IN THE KITCHEN * Add sprigs of curry to rice, vegetables, and deviled eggs.

PLANT NOTES * Don't confuse the curry plant with curry powder, which is a blend of several spices including turmeric, cumin, mustard seed, and fenugreek, among others. The plant cannot be used to replace the powder. * Curry may be grown for its scent. The essential oil is used to enhance fruit-flavoured confections and perfumes.

curry

daylilies

Hemerocallis spp.

Perennial

Height 25–120 cm; spread 60–90 cm

An upright, arching, grassy plant with large black, purple, mahogany, red, orange, yellow, pink, or cream-coloured blooms atop slender stems.

IN THE KITCHEN ✽ Petals and flower buds alike may be eaten; they have a crisp, fresh taste and are commonly used in soups, salads, and stir fries. They may also be cooked and eaten as a vegetable.

PLANT NOTES ✽ Daylilies have been cultivated for over 2,500 years.

Rack Of Lamb with Mint Crust

Use herbed bread crumbs to achieve different flavour effects. As you experiment with herbs, you'll discover new combinations and almost limitless possibilities!
—John

2	2	racks of lamb, 8 ribs each
2 tbsp.	30 mL	Dijon-style grain mustard
2 tbsp.	30 mL	honey
4 tbsp.	60 mL	finely chopped mint leaves
2 cups	500 mL	fine white bread crumbs
2 tbsp.	30 mL	melted butter *or* margarine
salt and pepper, to taste		

Preheat oven to 450°F (230°C). Line a roasting pan or baking sheet with foil. Trim racks of any excess fat; place on baking sheet. In a small bowl, mix together the mustard, honey, and mint; set aside. In a medium bowl, mix together the bread crumbs and melted butter; season with salt and pepper. Spread the mustard-honey mixture over the racks. Divide the bread-crumb mixture over the racks, pressing down slightly to form a crust. Bake racks for 30 minutes (medium rare), or to desired doneness. Allow the racks to stand at room temperature for 10 minutes. Slice the racks between the bones. Serve with fresh mint sauce (below).

Fresh Mint Sauce

3 tbsp.	45 mL	cold water
1½ tsp.	7 mL	icing sugar
⅓ cup	85 mL	vinegar
⅓ cup	85 mL	chopped fresh mint

In a small saucepan, heat water and sugar; stir to dissolve. Add vinegar and mint. Remove from heat and allow to stand at room temperature 1 hour before serving.

sweet rocket

Hesperis matronalis

Hardy biennial

Height 60–90 cm

Sweet rocket produces fragrant mauve, pink, purple, or white flowers atop tall, narrow stems with green lance-shaped leaves.

IN THE KITCHEN * Sweet rocket's flowers and leaves may be used in salads (although the flavour of the leaves is fairly strong—use sparingly). The flowers may be used as a garnish.

roselle

(Sudanese tea, red tea, Jamaica tea)

Hibiscus sabdariffa

Tender perennial

Height to 2.5 m; spread to 2 m

Woody perennial with lobed leaves and pale yellow or white flowers.

IN THE KITCHEN * Roselle leaves may be eaten raw or cooked; they are similar to rhubarb stalks in flavour. The seeds may also be roasted and eaten. Roselle is used to add acidic flavouring to sauces, jams, drinks, wines, curries, chutneys, and teas.

hyssop

Hyssopus officinalis

Perennial

Height 45–60 cm; spread 60–90 cm

Characterized by long, dense spikes of tubular, purple-blue, pink, or white flowers.

IN THE KITCHEN * Use leaves on legumes or meat dishes (especially game meat) in small amounts: the sage-mint flavour is slightly bitter. Good in soups, stews, and salads. The entire flower is edible and makes a lovely—and spicy— garnish. Hyssop oil is used in French dressing.

PLANT NOTES * Hyssop is used to flavour liqueurs like Chartreuse and Benedictine. * Hyssop makes a lovely ornamental. * Some people believe that hyssop will kill whitefly when planted near cabbage and will increase yields when planted near grapes.

hyssop

bay laurel

bay laurel

(bay, sweet bay)

Laurus nobilis

Tender perennial

Height to 3 m; spread to 1 m
when grown indoors

An aromatic evergreen tree with
shiny grey bark and shiny, dark-
green, elliptical leaves.

IN THE KITCHEN ❋ Bay complements soups, stews, tomato sauces,
seafood dishes, pickles, custards,
and rice puddings. Drop a leaf
into a jar of rice to inbue a mild
flavour.

PLANT NOTES ❋ Bay laurel makes
a wonderful potted tree, although
it must be brought indoors for the
winter in cool climates. Indoors,
bay laurel should be placed in a
sunny, cool spot (10–15°C) and
kept slightly dry. Bay laurel can be
pruned to different forms to suit
your taste. ❋ All laurels but this one
are poisonous. ❋ A symbol of glory
and reward, bay laurel garlands were
presented to champions of the first
Olympic Games in 776 BC.

Herbal Potpourri

*Stir frequently to release the
fragrance of this herbal potpourri.*
— *Joyce*

1 cup	250 mL	dried mint
2 cups	500 mL	dried marigolds
1 cup	250 mL	dried chrysanthe-mums
1 cup	250 mL	mixed herbs
(thyme, savory, marjoram, etc.)		
1	1	orange, thinly sliced, dried
1	1	lemon, thinly sliced, dried
A few	A few	dried chilies
4	4	large cinnamon sticks
2	2	whole nutmegs
4	4	star anise
1 tsp.	5 mL	mint essential oil (optional)
1 tbsp.	15 mL	orange essential oil (optional)

Combine all ingredients in a very
large plastic bag. If you use the
essential oils, be very careful: they
can damage wood and plastic
surfaces. Allow mixture to mature
for at least 1 week. Arrange in your
favourite bowl.
Hint❋ Make your own varieties by
adding special tea, mulling spices,
tiny dried pine cones, or different
spices. Potpourris must be kept out
of the reach of small children if the
essential oils are used.

garden cress

(pepperweed)

Lepidum sativum

Annual

Height 20–80 cm

Garden cress has a single erect
stem with lobed leaves and small,
almost spherical flowers; a curled
variety is available.

IN THE KITCHEN ✳ Garden cress
resembles watercress in taste; it is
known for its fresh, peppery flavour.
The leaves may be employed fresh
in salads, soups, sandwiches, and
omelettes. It also makes a nice
garnish for meat dishes.

lovage

(love parsley)

Levisticum officinale

Perennial

Height to 2 m; spread to 1 m

Lovage has smooth, very long
leaves (70 cm) and tiny, yellow-
green flowers.

IN THE KITCHEN ✳ Lovage
shoots are blanched and eaten as a
vegetable; their flavour is similar to
celery. The stalks are often used in
Bloody Marys. Seeds are added to
breads, cheese, biscuits, meat, and
crackers. Leaves are added to soups,
stews, and salads.

PLANT NOTES ✳ Lovage flowers
attract tiny, parasitic wasps that
prey on caterpillars.

sea parsley

(sea lovage)

Ligusticum scotium

Perennial

Height 5–90 cm; spread 10–60 cm

Sea parsley has red-green stems
and glossy leaves, divided into
three leaflets; green-white
flowers appear on umbels later
in the season.

IN THE KITCHEN ✳ Young leaves
and stalks have a pungent, celery-
like flavour. They may be eaten
raw or cooked, or may be added
to soups and stews. Peel back the
stem before eating or cooking.

PLANT NOTES ✳ The roots can
be chewed as a tobacco substitute
or used to scent bathwater.

honeysuckle

Lonicera caprifolium

Perennial

Height to 6 m; spread to 1.2 m

This creeping vine has dark-green,
lance-shaped leaves and produces
open-faced, tubular flowers that
start off pink and fade to white
or cream as the season passes.

IN THE KITCHEN ✳ The flowers
are aromatic and taste wonderful
in fruit salads. They also make a
nice syrup.

PLANT NOTES ✳ Honeysuckle
is a prolific bloomer and will bear
flowers to the very end of the
season. ✳ Honeysuckle flowers
are attractive to hummingbirds.

puffball

Lycoperdon perlatum

Annual

Height 3–9 cm; spread 3–6 cm

Pear- or club-shaped fungi with
warty skin; they start off white,
then turn yellow-brown.

IN THE KITCHEN ✳ Young, white
puffballs can be eaten fresh or fried
in batter.

PLANT NOTES ✳ Puffballs were
used in traditional Native American and Chinese medicine. ✳ My
sons, Bill and Jim, used to pick
puffballs from between rows of
potatoes so that I could fry them.

mallow

mallow

Malva verticillata crispa

Annual

Height 45–90 cm; spread 60–90 cm

Lobed leaves and pale, purple-pink
flowers with dark veins.

IN THE KITCHEN ✳ Young leaves
and shoots may be eaten raw in
salads or cooked with vegetables.
The unripe seed capsules (called
"cheeses" because of their unusual
shape) are delicious in salads.

PLANT NOTES ✳ Mallow makes
a pretty ornamental.

Herbal Marinades

*Use the dill-mustard marinade with
halibut, salmon, tuna, and swordfish
steaks. Try fruity orange-thyme
marinade with chicken and pork.*
—John

Dill-Mustard Marinade

⅓ cup	85 mL	Dijon-style grain mustard
⅓ cup	85 mL	lemon juice
3	3	garlic cloves, crushed
2 tbsp.	30 mL	chopped dill
salt and freshly ground black pepper, to taste		
1 cup	250 mL	olive oil

In a glass bowl, mix the mustard,
lemon juice, garlic, dill, salt, and
pepper. Whisk in the olive oil,
mixing until marinade is well
combined. Marinate fish 2 to 3
hours, covered, in the refrigerator.
Discard any leftover marinade.

Orange-Thyme Marinade

1 cup	250 mL	orange juice
⅓ cup	85 mL	honey
⅓ cup	85 mL	balsamic vinegar
1	1	medium onion, diced
4		garlic cloves, crushed
1 tbsp.	15 mL	orange rind, grated
1 tbsp.	15 mL	chopped thyme
½ tsp.	2.5 mL	ground cloves
½ tsp.	2.5 mL	ground ginger

In a glass bowl, combine all
ingredients. Marinate meat overnight; reserve marinade to brush
over meat when cooking. Discard
any leftover marinade.

horehound

(white horehound)

Marrubium vulgare

Perennial

Height 20–60 cm; spread 20–60 cm

Distinguished by velvety grey-green leaves with serrated edges.

IN THE KITCHEN * Pungent, even bitter, horehound is used as flavouring for soups, salads, fish, chicken, ale, and even candy for sore throats.

PLANT NOTES * Horehound attracts bees and has been used as a cure for canker worm in trees. * The Romans used to place a horehound plant in milk in an attempt to rid their houses of flies.

alfalfa

Medicago sativa

Perennial

Height 30–90 cm; Spread 15–60 cm

A bushy plant, alfalfa has 3-lobed, toothed, oval leaves and small purple-to-lilac flowers.

IN THE KITCHEN * Leaves may be consumed raw or cooked as a vegetable. Seed sprouts, with their pea-like flavour, may be added liberally to salads or sandwiches.

PLANT NOTES * Alfalfa, native to central Asia, arrived in North America as a forage crop; it is now found growing wild in almost every province and state, having escaped cultivation.

beebalm

(bergamot, Oswego tea)

Monarda didyma

Perennial

Height 45–120 cm; spread 30–60 cm

Beebalm has ovate, toothed leaves and bright-green flowers with red-green bracts.

IN THE KITCHEN * The large, strongly flavoured flowers—in white, pink, purple, or red—taste of citrus, thyme, or mint. Cut flowers as soon as they are fully open. They can be added, fresh or dried, to salads, pork, chicken, pasta, vegetables, or fish. Use sparingly to avoid overpowering the flavour of the dish. The leaves may be infused as tea; the flavour is reminiscent of Earl Grey.

PLANT NOTES * Beebalm flower colour and flavour keeps beautifully when dried or preserved in oil or vinegar. Kept in an airtight jar, dried flowers will keep up to 3 months. * Beebalm has an orange scent, making it a good choice for potpourris. It also makes a wonderful border plant, and, of course, it attracts bees.

sweet cicely

(British myrrh, sugar saver)

Myrrhis odorata

Perennial

Height 60–90 cm; spread 60–120 cm

Sweet cicely has fern-like leaves up to 50 cm long and tiny, sweet-scented white flowers atop large but delicate umbels.

IN THE KITCHEN * Sweet cicely is often called the "sugar herb" because of the high saccharine content of its leaves. Young flowers and leaves alike are very sweet, with an aniseed flavour. Leaves and flowers may be added to soups, stews, wine cups, and tart fruit-dishes like gooseberries, plums, apples, and rhubarb. It's also a low-calorie sweetener for whipped cream, yogourt, and stewed fruit. Sweet cicely's roots may be eaten raw in salads or cooked as a vegetable. The seeds make a nice addition to salads.

PLANT NOTES * Sweet cicely is one of the few plants that likes shade. It makes a pretty ornamental in a shade bed.

Mint Cup

Reminiscent of the ever-popular Pimms Cup, but without the alcohol.
—Joyce

4	4	large springs of mint
1 tsp.	5 mL	sugar
crushed ice		
1 tsp.	5 mL	fresh lemon juice
3 tbsp.	45 mL	"Roses" lime cordial
chilled tonic		
cucumber *or* lemon slices		
mint sprigs		

Muddle the mint sprigs and sugar in a glass or wine goblet. (If you don't have a muddler in your home bar, use the end of a wooden spoon or a mortar and pestle.) Add the crushed ice, stir again, then add the lemon juice, cordial, and tonic. Stir gently and garnish with cucumber slices and mint sprigs. Serve immediately. To make ahead of time, prepare mint and sugar mixture in each goblet. Cover and refrigerate for up to 8 hours. Makes 1.

Sorrel Tea

Enjoy the flavours of summer even in the heart of winter.
—John

4 cups	1 L	water
½ cup	125 mL	dried sorrel
2	2	whole cloves
3-inch	7.5-cm	piece of cinnamon stick
3 tbsp.	45 mL	granulated sugar

In a saucepan, combine the ingredients. Bring the water to a boil. Remove from the heat. Cover with a lid and steep for 10 minutes. Strain and serve hot.

Greek myrtle

Myrtus communis

Tender perennial

Height 2–3 m; spread to 3 m

An erect shrub with dark-green, aromatic, ovate leaves and wide white flowers with yellow stamens; blue-black berries follow later in the summer.

IN THE KITCHEN * The spicy leaves may be used in pork, lamb, stuffing, fish, or game meat dishes. They are often used like bay leaves, fresh or dried. The dried flower buds and fruit can be crushed and used like peppercorns.

PLANT NOTES
* In cooler climates, Greek myrtle is best grown in containers. Give it full sun and lots of water. * Greek myrtle is an attractive, aromatic ornamental and makes a very nice houseplant. It is a good bonsai plant for beginners.

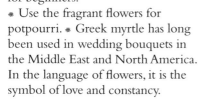

* Use the fragrant flowers for potpourri. * Greek myrtle has long been used in wedding bouquets in the Middle East and North America. In the language of flowers, it is the symbol of love and constancy.

watercress

Nasturtium officinale

Perennial

Height 10–60 cm; spread indefinite

An aquatic perennial, watercress has floating stems with small, dark green, oval leaves and bears tiny white flowers all summer long.

IN THE KITCHEN * Leaves may be added fresh to salads or used in herb butter. Watercress may also be included in soups or fish sauces.

catnip

Nepeta cataria

Perennial

Height 30–100 cm; spread 25–60 cm

Catnip has large, serrated leaves and small white or pink (sometimes blue or lilac), red- or purple-spotted flowers.

IN THE KITCHEN * Most commonly employed in teas, catnip leaves may also be chopped up for sauces, soups, pastas, grains, and vegetables. The young leaf shoots are tasty sprinkled on salads.

PLANT NOTES * Catnip is most famous for its euphoria-inducing effect on cats. For those concerned that they could turn their cats into drug addicts by exposing their pets to the plant, there's no need to fear. Scientists have found no evidence that catnip harms cats. * Early American hangmen often ate catnip root before they were to report for duty. Common wisdom at the time held that the root could make even the most gentle person turn mean. Thus, consuming the root helped hangmen steel themselves for the unpleasant task that lay before them.

evening primrose

(evening star)

Oenothera biennis

Hardy biennial

Height 90–120 cm; spread to 90 cm

Bears long, green, oval- or lance-shaped leaves and large, fluorescent, yellow flowers that bloom for most of the summer.

IN THE KITCHEN ✳ The roots,

evening primrose

leaves, flower buds, whole flowers, and stems of evening primrose may all be eaten. If boiled, the roots resemble parsnips in flavour and texture. They can be pickled and used as an aperitif. Remove the green bits before eating the flowers. The yellow flowers look and taste great in salads.

PLANT NOTES ✳ When night falls, the flowers are fragrant and emit a phosphorescent glow. ✳ *Similar species:* Ozark sundrops (*Oenothera macrocarpa*) is a low-growing evening primrose, but only the petals of this variety are edible.

Minted Pea Sauce

Excellent with grilled or roast lamb, grilled chicken, or veal.
—John

1½ cups	375 mL	chicken broth, bouillon, *or* chicken stock
2½ cups	625 mL	frozen baby peas
¾ cup	175 mL	fresh mint leaves, packed
1 tsp.	sugar	5 mL
2 tbsp.	30 mL	margarine *or* butter
salt and white pepper, to taste		

In a medium saucepan over medium-high heat, bring chicken stock to a boil. Add 2 cups (500 mL) of the peas (reserve ½ cup/125 mL). Add the mint leaves, sugar, and margarine; cook uncovered on medium heat for 5 minutes. Cool mixture for 10 minutes. In a blender or food processor, purée the cooled mixture until smooth. Season with salt and pepper to taste. Strain the sauce through a fine sieve into a clean saucepan. Add remaining peas and cook gently for 2 to 3 minutes over medium heat. Serve immediately.

poppy

poppy

(corn poppy, Flanders poppy,
field poppy)

Papaver rhoeas

Annual; sows seed readily

Height 40–60 cm; spread 10–45 cm

Hairy, slender stems each bear a
single, dark-centred red flower.

IN THE KITCHEN ✳ Poppy seeds
are commonly used in breads,
cookies, rolls, cakes, biscuits, and
pastries to add texture and a mild,
nutty flavour. Poppy seed oil is
often used in cooking.

PLANT NOTES ✳ Poppies are
lovely and look wonderful grouped
in flowerbeds, borders, mass
plantings, edgings, backgrounds,
containers, and meadow gardens.
✳ One of the most recognized
flowers in the world, poppies have
become a symbol of sacrifice and
valour since the First World War.

passion flower
(maypop)

Passiflora incarnata
or *Passiflora edulis*

Annual

Height to 8 m; spread indefinite

Long, trailing vine bears star-like,
lavender flowers that develop
into edible fruits.

IN THE KITCHEN ✳ Passion flower
fruits are pulped for jams and jellies,
sherbets, drinks, and tonics.

PLANT NOTES ✳ Passion flower
should be grown in your warmest,
sunniest window or in a greenhouse. It needs a support like a
trellis to grow upon. ✳ Spanish
missionaries in South America saw
these pretty flowers as symbols of
Christ's passion; hence the name.
✳ Passion flower was an popular cure
for insomnia in the 19th century.

lemon geranium
Pelargonium crispum

Annual

Height 30–100 cm; spread 30–45 cm

Lemon geranium has rough,
crinkled, serrated, rounded, or
lobed leaves about 1 cm in
length.

IN THE KITCHEN ✳ The leaves
may be infused to make tea or
used fresh to add lemon flavour to
sauces, sorbets, ice cream, cakes,
fruit punch, gelatins, vinegar, and

pudding. The flowers are also edible, but not nearly as tasty as the leaves; however, they add a lovely visual component to dishes.

PLANT NOTES * Lemon geranium is best grown in pots. I plant scented geraniums of all kinds on my deck for the wonderful fragrance. * Lemon geraniums (indeed, all scented geraniums) were very popular for flavouring food during the Victorian era and are enjoying a resurgence today. * Dried lemon geranium leaves may be used in potpourris and herb pillows. * One drop of scented geranium oil to 2 tsp. (10 mL) of almond oil makes a good treatment for dry skin. * Lemon geraniums originated in South Africa. * According to the Victorian language of flowers, lemon geraniums signify "an unexpected meeting."

perilla

(green shiso, Japanese basil, aoshiso)

Perilla frutescens var. *crispa*

Annual

Height 60–120 cm; spread 30–60 cm

Bushy, attractive plant with deeply veined masses of oval, crinkled, slightly aromatic leaves and small white flowers.

IN THE KITCHEN * Shiso has a lovely, sweet, light, spicy flavour. Fresh or pickled leaves and seeds are used in tempura, pickles, sushi, and bean curd; the herb is widely used in Asian cuisine. Young leaves and shoots are delicious fried in butter. The flowers add subtle flavour to salad dressings and stir-fry dishes.

More Easy Ways to Use Herbs and Edible Flowers

* Lay skinned chicken pieces on a bed of long stems of thyme, savory, marjoram, and mint. Brush with a mixture of honey and Dijon mustard. Turn frequently while baking.

* Sprinkle fat slices of fresh tomatoes with olive oil, basil, savory, and thyme, then lots of freshly ground pepper.

* Herb blossoms add wonderful flavour and colour to omelettes, crepes, and specialty egg, cheese, or fish entrees. Try chives, garlic chives, sage, oregano, savory, thyme, oregano, and borage.

* Add rosemary and mint to your favourite lemonade. Refrigerate at least 2 hours before serving.

* Prepare a fresh petal salad by starting with leaf lettuce, tiny spinach, and borage leaves. Then add a selection of pineapple sage blossoms, silver thyme blossoms, rose petals, or nasturtium. Keep colour and flavour in mind, and use a dressing of a single oil and fresh lemon juice.

* Add savory, thyme, and sage to your next batch of crabapple or red currant jelly. Wonderful with pork, poultry, liver, or macaroni and cheese.

* Dry bunches of herbs to put into dried flower arrangements, wreaths, Christmas trees, or special parcels. Thyme, sage, rosemary, savory, lavender, oregano, and chamomile are all good choices.

PLANT NOTES ✳ *Similar species:*
red shiso (*Perilla frutescens* var. *crispa
rubra),* also called akashiso or purple
shiso, has pink flowers, a nice
complement to the red/purple
leaves. The striking red/purple
variety is best used for pickling,
especially for adding red colour
to pickled plums or ginger. Or
chop red shiso very finely and
add to salad and rice dishes.
✳ Green shiso makes a pretty
ornamental. Constant picking
of flowers will promote leafy
growth.

anise

green shiso

anise

Pimpinella anisum

Annual

Height to 50 cm; spread 25–50 cm

Anise produces tiny, off-white
flowers on attractive umbels.

IN THE KITCHEN ✳ Anise's
licorice-flavoured leaves are often
employed in salads. The seeds
flavour candy, dried figs, cakes,
breads, and curries. The seeds and
leaves may also be used to make
licorice tea.

PLANT NOTES ✳ When chewed,
the seeds and leaves freshen the
breath. ✳ Anise is employed in eau
de Cologne. ✳ Anise has long been
considered an aphrodisiac.

Vietnamese coriander

(rau ram, Vietnamese cilantro, Vietnamese parsley)

Polygonum odoratum

Tender perennial

Height 30–45 cm; spread indefinite

Green and red-marked, lance-shaped leaves on long red stems.

IN THE KITCHEN ✳ Vietnamese coriander has a lemon/coriander scent and tastes like cilantro, only milder. It may be added to meat dishes, especially chicken and turkey. The young leaves may be used in green salads and potato salads.

French purslane

(garden purslane, green purslane)

Portulaca oleracea var. *sativa*

Annual

Height 20–45 cm; spread 45–60 cm

Garden purslane has succulent, spoon-shaped leaves, about 3 cm in length.

IN THE KITCHEN ✳ French purslane is a traditional ingredient in French soups and Middle Eastern salads like fattoush. Its flavour can be rather sharp. The stems and leaves can be pickled.

PLANT NOTES ✳ Similar species: Golden purslane (*Portulaca oleracea* var. *aurea*) is also edible and has gold-tinted foliage that contrasts nicely with other greens. ✳ Purslane is well suited to heavily compacted soils and very poor soils. It is also drought tolerant. Purslane is a prolific seed producer—even when cut from the roots, the plant will continue to produce seed. ✳ At night, purslane absorbs carbon dioxide, which attaches to acids in the plant. The plant needs several hours of morning sunlight to convert the carbon dioxide to sugars and release the acids. So purslane picked first thing in the morning will be bitter—wait until afternoon to harvest it.

French purslane

salad burnet

cowslip primrose

salad burnet

(garden burnet)

Poterium sanguisorba

Perennial

Height to 90 cm

A bushy herb, salad burnet has central stems with 7 to 11 plump, rounded leaflets.

IN THE KITCHEN ✳ Salad burnet's nutty, cucumber flavour adds spice to soups, casseroles, cream cheese, herb vinegars, and salads (especially with mayonnaise or French dressing). The fresh leaves are terrific in coleslaw.

PLANT NOTES ✳ Salad burnet serves as a pretty ornamental in a mixed border or as an edging plant in a formal border. ✳ Salad burnet has been used medicinally for at least 2000 years, often as a facial. ✳ The species name, *sanguisorba*, means "blood ball."

primrose

Primula vulgaris

Perennial

Height 15 cm; spread 15 cm

Low mounding plant with deeply wrinkled, ovate leaves and small, bright-yellow, 5-petalled flowers.

IN THE KITCHEN ✳ Primrose flowers add flavour and colour to green salads, and they may be candied to decorate desserts. The flowers may also be used for tea. The young leaves may be steamed and served buttered.

PLANT NOTES ✳ ***Similar species:*** cowslip (*Primula veris*) flowers may be used in the same manner as primroses.

rhubarb

rhubarb

Rheum x *cultorum*

Perennial

Height up to 2 m; spread indefinite

Long, thick red or green stalks and huge, crinkled, dark green leaves.

IN THE KITCHEN ✳ A northern standard, rhubarb is used in pies, punch, pudding, jam, jelly, relish, cake, tarts, and ice cream. My daughter-in-law Valerie sometimes treats us to rhubarb pork. The tart stalks may be eaten raw, alone or dipped in sugar, for a mouth-watering treat.

PLANT NOTES ✳ Do not eat rhubarb leaves. They contain oxalic acid, which is poisonous. Rhubarb stalks should be cooked in stainless steel, not copper, iron, or aluminum pots. ✳ The term "rhubarb" (an argument or dispute) seems to have originated on the baseball diamond. Brooklyn Dodgers announcer "Red" Barber first used it in 1943 to describe an altercation between players.

elder

Sambucus nigra

Perennial

Height 4.5–10 m; spread 3.5–4.5 m

Large, showy deciduous shrub with corky, grey-brown bark and tiny, scented, cream-coloured flowers that are followed by black berries.

IN THE KITCHEN ✳ Elder flowers may be made into fritters. The berries may be made into sauces, jams, jellies, sorbets, cordial, and wine.

PLANT NOTES ✳ In the fall, cook the berries slightly before using them. ✳ Elders are grown primarily for their magnificent foliage, which adds colour and texture to yards and gardens. ✳ It is said that before an elder is pruned, permission should be asked of the shrub to avoid offending the spirits within. According to myth, elders will never be struck by lightning and will protect the home from "evil influences."

chickweed

Stellaria media

Annual

Height 5–40 cm; spread 5–40 cm

Low-growing plant with minute, ovate leaves and white, star-shaped flowers.

IN THE KITCHEN * Chickweed sprigs may be added to salads or steamed lightly and served as a leafy vegetable.

PLANT NOTES * Chickweed spreads rapidly, tolerates shade, and loves cool, moist areas and rich soil. Many gardeners consider it a weed (it's certainly the bane of our garden!), but it makes a lovely pot-herb if kept confined. * Chickweed sprigs are often fed to pet birds.

chickweed

stevia

Stevia rebaudiana

Tender perennial

Height 30–60 cm

A slender perennial herb with long, weak, semi-woody stems and purple-and-white flowers.

IN THE KITCHEN * The powdered leaf may be used as a sugar substitute in drinks and baked desserts.

PLANT NOTES * Stevia is hundreds of times sweeter than sucrose, making it a superb low-calorie sugar substitute. * Indigenous peoples in Paraguay and Brazil have used stevia as a sweetener for centuries, and during World War Two, stevia was cultivated as a possible sugar substitute.

costmary

(bible leaf, alecost)

Tanacetum balsamita

Perennial

Height to 80 cm; spread to 60 cm

Bears oblong, sweetly scented, silver-green leaves and clusters of daisy-like flowers on long stalks.

IN THE KITCHEN * Leaves may be added to salads, sauces, soups, meat and vegetable dishes. It also makes a good tea. Leaves should be pinched before flowering. Costmary's flavour is fairly strong—use it sparingly.

PLANT NOTES * Costmary makes a pretty ornamental and repels insects. It is also useful in potpourris, sachets, and herb wreaths and pillows.

dandelion

Taraxacum officinale

Very hardy perennial

Height 15–20 cm

Common, yellow-flowered, bristly leafed plant with bright-yellow, single-stemmed flowers.

IN THE KITCHEN ❋ Almost all parts of the dandelion can be eaten. The greens make an excellent substitute for spinach: they are high in vitamins A and C, and contain high levels of iron, calcium, phosphorus, potassium, magnesium, and copper. Add dandelion leaves and bacon to green salads—the combined flavours are lovely! Leaves are best eaten in early spring; they turn bitter in late spring and summer. The crowns can be deep-fried. The roots can be roasted and ground as a coffee substitute. Young buds are high in protein. Pick flowers as you need them and only use fresh. Cut flowers as close to the head as possible; remove the stem and green bits. The flowers close up almost immediately after you pick them; to prevent this, put them in a bowl of water and pluck them out just before you eat them or toss them into your salad. Fry flowers in a little bit of butter and serve immediately—wonderful for breakfast! Dandelion flowers can also be used to make wine.

PLANT NOTES ❋ Never eat dandelions that may have been in contact with lawn fertilizers, herbicides, or other contaminants. ❋ Cultivated varieties like 'Thick-Leaved Improved' and 'Verte de Montgomery' are better for eating than wild dandelions, which can be bitter and tough. ❋ Dandelions produce viable seed without pollination, can grow at elevations as high as 3000 m, and last from the first sign of spring until autumn. ❋ Eaten for centuries in Eurasia, dandelions were brought to North America as a pot-herb. The Arabs have used them for medicinal purposes since the 10th century, while in Victorian England dandelions were often grown as a salad herb. ❋ During World War Two, dandelions were cultivated for the latex extracted from the roots. The latex was used to make rubber.

dandelion

red clover
Trifolium pratense

Annual

Height 20–60 cm; spread indefinite

Long, 3-lobed leaves and densely packed, globular pink flower heads atop slender stems.

IN THE KITCHEN * Red clover may be employed in soups, salads, teas, dressings, baked goods, and pickling. Break the flower heads into individual petals and sprinkle lightly over dishes. Use in moderation: clover can be difficult to digest.

PLANT NOTES * Originally introduced to North America as a forage plant, red clover has escaped from cultivation and can be found growing wild across Canada and the northern United States. * A legume, red clover grows best in moderately cool to warm smmer temperatures.

fenugreek
Trigonella foenum-graecum

Annual

Height to 60 cm; spread 30–45 cm

Fenugreek bears trifoliate leaves and yellow-white flowers (violet-tinged at the base); flowers are followed by yellow-brown seeds.

IN THE KITCHEN * Dried leaves are often used to flavour root vegetables in Indian and Middle Eastern cooking. Ground fenugreek seeds are a common ingredient in curry powder. Roasted seeds may be used as a coffee substitute; seed sprouts and fresh leaves can be eaten as vegetables.

PLANT NOTES * Fenugreek is used commercially for making imitation maple, vanilla, caramel and butterscotch flavours. * In Ethiopia and Egypt, fenugreek seeds are used to flavour bread.

stinging nettle
Urtica dioica

Perennial

Height to 1.5 m; spread indefinite

Nettle bears toothy, ovate leaves, covered with bristly hairs that may be abrasive and painful to the touch.

IN THE KITCHEN * The young leaf tips and young shoots may be cooked like spinach or puréed for soup. Never eat the raw leaves whole: the stinging bristles would make such an experience extremely painful. Eat only the young leaves: old leaves can contain high levels of oxalic acid.

PLANT NOTES * To avoid the leaf spines, wear gloves when harvesting and preparing, and pick at the base of the stem. * Nettle is very rich in iron. * Nettle was used in manufacturing cloth—the word nettle means "twist," as in to make fibre.

Lavender Cake with White Chocolate

1 18-oz. package	1 510-g package	white cake mix
1 3-oz. package	92-g package	vanilla instant pudding
1 cup	250 mL	sour cream
¼ cup	50 mL	mayonnaise
½ cup	125 mL	oil
½ cup	125 mL	lavender infusion
1 tsp.	5 mL	pure vanilla
½ tsp.	2 mL	rose essence (optional)
8-oz. package	225-g package	white chocolate chips
or		
1½ cups	375 mL	chopped white chocolate
lavender icing sugar		

To make the lavender infusion, put ½ cup (125 mL) lavender stems and/or seeds in a small bowl. Cover with ¾ cup (175 mL) boiling water and let stand 4 to 6 hours or until a strong infusion develops. Strain out stems/seeds. Makes ¾ cup (175 mL); discard excess infusion. Grease a 10-inch (25-cm) bundt pan thoroughly with shortening or unsalted butter. Combine all ingredients except chocolate and icing sugar in a large bowl. Blend ingredients slowly with mixer and then beat on medium speed for 2 minutes. Stir in chocolate. Pour or spoon into bundt pan. Bake at 350°F (175°C) for 50 minutes or until cake tests done. Cool on rack 10 minutes before removing from pan. Cool completely. Place on serving dish and wrap tightly in double plastic wrap. For best flavour and moistness, allow the cake to stand at room temperature 12 to 48 hours before serving. Just before serving, dust with lavender icing sugar and garnish with a few lavender stems. Serves 12.

Lavender Icing Sugar❋ Spoon a small amount of icing sugar into a dish or bottle. Add several lavender sprigs. Cover tightly and set aside to develop flavour. (Flavour may be achieved quickly by using a mortar and pestle.) Sift to remove stems. Note❋ Do not use commercial lavender seeds in cooking as they are generally treated and are not meant for consumption.

Variation❋ Cake may also be made by substituting lemon-scented or rose-scented geranium leaves for lavender.

A scrumptious summer cake to serve with iced Earl Grey Tea. Garnish with a touch of whipped cream and slices of luscious fresh peaches.
—Joyce

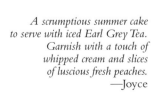

wasabi

(Japanese horseradish)

Wasabia japonica

Perennial

Height 20–40 cm; spread to 30 cm

Each upright stem is topped with a single kidney-shaped leaf; stems bear small white flowers in summer.

IN THE KITCHEN * Wasabi's roots are ground like horseradish; they add fiery taste to meat and fish dishes. Wasabi may also be blended into dip.

PLANT NOTES * Wasabi is probably best known to North Americans as the condiment served with sushi, but it has many other uses.

ginger

Zingiber officinale

Perennial

Height 1.5 m; spread indefinite

Ginger has upright stems with long, pointed, lance-shaped leaves and yellow-green flowers with a deep purple, yellow-stained lip.

IN THE KITCHEN * Ginger is used in chutneys, meat and fish dishes, soups, marinades, and curries. Fresh young rhizomes can be eaten raw or preserved in syrup and candied. When dried and ground, ginger spices up cakes, sauces, and cookies—including the ever-popular ginger snaps, which my husband Ted adores.

PLANT NOTES * Add ginger to the tub for a refreshing, tingly bath. * In India, ginger and cinnamon are combined to make tea.

Inedible Plant Species

As we have said throughout this book, it is important that you be sure you know which plants are safe to eat and which plants are not. Here is a partial list of plants you must **never** eat. Remember, if you are at all unsure about the identity of a species, err on the side of caution. Do not use any part of a plant unless you are certain you have identified it correctly and know it is edible.

Aconitum napellus
   monkshood, aconite, wolfsbane

Acorus calamus
   calamus, sweet root, sweet cane,
   sweet cinnamon, sweet flag,
   calamus, myrtle flag

Actaea spicata
   baneberry

Aesculus hippocasteranum
   buckeyes,
   aesculus horse chestnut

Aethusa cynapium
   fool's parsley

Agrostemma githago
   corncockle

Anemone **spp.**
   all anemone species

Aquilegia vulgaris
   columbine

Arnica montana
   arnica, arnica flowers, leopard's-
   bane, wolf's-bane, flores arnicae,
   mountain tobacco

Artemisia absinthium
   wormwood, absinthe absinthium,
   absint madderwort, wermut
   mugwort, mingwort, warmot

Arum maculatum
   lords and ladies

Atropa belladonna
   belladonna, deadly nightshade

Bryonia dioica
   white, red bryony,
   English mandrake

Buxus **spp.**
   all box species

Caltha palustris
   marsh marigold

Colchicum autumnale
   meadow saffron, autumn crocus

Conium maculatum
   hemlock, conium, poison hemlock,
   spotted hemlock, spotted parsley,
   St. Bennet's herb, spotted cowbane,
   fool's parsley

Convallaria majalis
   lily of the valley,
   convallaria, may lily

Corynanthe yohimbi
   yohimbe, yohimbi

Cytisus scoparius
   broom-tops, scoparius,
   spartium irish broom

Datura stramonium
   jimson weed stramonium, apple peru,
   jamestown thornapple, tolgause

Digitalis purpurea
   foxglove

Dipteryx odorata
   tonka bean, tonco bean, tonquin
   bean (aka *Coumarouna odorata*,
   Dipteryx oppositifolia,
   Coumarouna oppositifolia)

Euonymus atropurpureus
   wahoo bark, wahoo euonymus,
   burning bush

Euonymus europaeus
   spindle tree and other
   species of *Euonymus*

Eupatorium rugosum
   white snakeroot, snakeroot,
   richweed (aka *Eupatorium
   ogeratoides*)

***Euphorbia* spp.**
all spurges

Exagonium purga
jalap root, jalap true jalap, vera cruz
jalap, high bentham, ipomoea nutt,
john root (aka *Exagonium jalapa*)

Hedera helix
ivy

Heliotropium eropaeum
heliotrope

Helleborus foetidus
stinking hellebore

Helleborus niger
Christmas/Lenten rose

Helleborus viridis
green hellebore

Hyacinthus orientalis
hyacinth

Hyoscyamus niger
henbane, black henbane, hogs bean,
devil's eye, poison tobacco

Hypericum perforatum
St. Johnswort, hypericum,
goatweed, klamath weed

Ipomoea purpurea
morning glory

***Iris* spp.**
all iris species

***Lathyrus* spp.**
all sweet pea species

Lobelia inflata
lobelia, Indian tobacco,
wild tobacco, asthma weed,
emetic weed

Ligustrum vulgare
privet

Mandragora officinarum
mandrake, mandragora,
European mandrake

Mercurialis perennis
dog's mercury

***Narcissus* spp.**
all daffodil species

Oenanthe crocata
water dropwort

Ornithogalum umbellatum
star of Bethlehem

Podophyllum peltatum
mandrake, podophyllum, may and
devil apple, american mandrake,
umbrella plant, vegetable calomel,
vegetable mercury, wild lemon

Phoradendron flavescens
mistletoe (aka *Viscum flavescens*)

Phoradendron juniperinum
mistletoe, viscum juniper mistletoe

Prunus laurocerasus
laurel, cherry laurel

***Ranunculus* spp.**
all buttercup and
celandine species

***Rhododendron azalea* ssp.**
all azalea species

Sanguinaris canadensis
bloodroot, red puccoon,
sanguinaria

Solanum dulcamara
bittersweet twigs dulcamara,
bittersweet, woody nightshade,
climbing nightshade

Solanum tuberosum
potato foliage & green tubers

***Vinca* spp.**
all periwinkle species

Viscum album
mistletoe,
viscum european mistletoe

***Wisteria* spp.**
all wisteria species

Appendix

Herbs and Edible Flowers to Grow from Seed

Most people grow herbs and edible flowers by transplanting large plants from the greenhouse, and this is what I recommend for the sake of ease and convenience. However, the following can be grown successfully from seed.

angelica (biennial)
anise (annual)
borage (annual)
calendula (annual)
caraway (biennial)
chamomile (annual)
chervil (annual)
chives (perennial)
cilantro (annual)
cumin (annual)
dill (annual)
fennel
   (annual in most parts of Canada)
lavender (perennial)
lemon balm
   (annual in most parts of Canada)

lovage
   (perennial; should only be grown from seed)
marjoram (annual)
mustards (annual)
nasturtium (annual)
parsley (annual)
roquette (annual)
rosemary (perennial)
sage (perennial)
salad burnet (perennial)
sorrel (perennial)
summer savory (annual)
sunflower (annual)
sweet cicely (perennial)
violets (annual)
winter savory (perennial)

When to Start Seed Indoors

"Last frost" refers to the date of the average last spring frost in your area. Remember to harden off young plants before moving them outside for the season.

VARIETY	WHEN TO START SEED	WHEN TO MOVE TO GARDEN
balm, lemon	8 weeks prior to last frost	when soil is warm enough to work
basil	3 to 4 weeks prior to last frost	2 to 3 weeks after last frost
fennel	6 weeks prior to last frost	around last frost
nasturtium	1 week prior to last frost	2 weeks after last frost
pansies	16 to 18 weeks prior to last frost	4 to 5 weeks before last frost
parsley	6 to 8 weeks prior to last frost	2 weeks before last frost
rosemary	7 weeks before last frost	2 weeks before last frost
sage	4 weeks prior to last frost	2 weeks after last frost
savory, summer	8 weeks prior to last frost	2 weeks after last frost
savory, winter	8 weeks prior to last frost	around average last frost
violets	16 to 18 weeks prior to last frost	4 to 5 weeks before last frost
violas	14 to 16 weeks prior to last frost	4 to 5 weeks before last frost

Herbs for Specific Locations

Herbs and Edible Flowers to Grow for Scent

Shade-tolerant herbs for outdoors

Partial shade is fine for these herbs, although they will be lusher if they receive full sun. Remember that "tolerates" means "puts up with," not "likes."
basil, bay, chervil, lemon balm, mint, parsley, sweet cicely, tarragon, woodruff

Herbs for a sunny window box or trough

calendula, chives, dill, lemon thyme, lemon verbena, marjoram, sage, savory, scented geranium, tarragon

Herbs for indoor gardens

Generally, the smaller species flourish indoors.
basil, bay, chives, parsley, rosemary, savory, sweet marjoram, tarragon, thyme

Best herbs and edible flowers for scent

basil, beebalm, chamomile, fennel, hyssop, lavender, lemon balm, lemon verbena, rosemary, scented geraniums, sweet marjoram, thyme

Best herbs and edible flowers for potpourri

bay, beebalm, cardamom, chamomile, cilantro, dianthus, Greek myrtle, lavender, lemon verbena, lemongrass, marjoram, mint, orange thyme, oregano, pansies, pineapple sage, rosemary, roses, scented geraniums

Best herbs and edible flowers for attracting bees

basil, borage, clover, hyssop, lemon balm, marjoram, rosemary, sage, savory, thyme

Complimentary Herbs for Common Foods

Asparagus: basil, chives, dill, tarragon

Beans, dried: coriander, cumin, garlic, marjoram, oregano, rosemary, sage, savory, tarragon, thyme

Beans, green: basil, bay leaf, dill, garlic, marjoram, rosemary, savory, tarragon, thyme

Beans, lima: basil, chives, dill, marjoram, sage, savory, tarragon

Beef: basil, bay leaf, garlic, ginger, marjoram, oregano, thyme

Beets: caraway seeds, chives, dill, ginger, horseradish

Cabbage family (broccoli, cauliflower, cabbage, brussels sprouts): basil, caraway seeds, garlic, ginger, marjoram, oregano, tarragon, thyme

Carrots: caraway seeds, chives, ginger, marjoram, tarragon

Chicken/turkey: basil, bay leaf, chives, coriander, garlic, ginger, marjoram, oregano, rosemary, sage, tarragon, thyme

Corn: chives, coriander, rosemary, sage, savory, thyme

Eggs: chives, savory, tarragon

Eggplant: basil, garlic, marjoram, oregano, sage, thyme

Fish: bay leaf, chives, coriander, dill, nutmeg, sage, tarragon, thyme

Lamb: dill, garlic, mint, oregano, rosemary, thyme

Mushrooms: basil, chives, dill, garlic, marjoram, oregano, rosemary, tarragon

Peas: basil, chives, dill, marjoram, mint, oregano, savory, tarragon

Peppers, sweet: chives, coriander, garlic, marjoram, oregano, thyme

Pork: caraway seeds, coriander, dill, garlic, ginger, rosemary, sage, thyme

Potatoes: caraway seeds, bay leaf, chives, coriander, dill, garlic, mint, oregano, tarragon, thyme

Rice: chives, garlic, sage, tarragon

Shellfish: bay leaf, basil, chervil, coriander, cloves, dill, marjoram, oregano, tarragon, thyme

Spinach: basil, garlic, tarragon

Squash, yellow and zucchini: basil, chives, coriander, dill, garlic, ginger, marjoram, oregano, rosemary, savory, tarragon

Tomatoes: basil, chives, coriander, dill, garlic, marjoram, oregano, rosemary, sage, savory, tarragon, thyme

Veal: bay leaf, coriander, dill, garlic, oregano, rosemary, sage, thyme

Bibliography

Culinary References

Bremness, L. *The Complete Book of Herbs*. New York: Reader's Digest Association (Canada Ltd.), 1989.

Butler, John. *A Treasury of Cookbook Classics*. Edmonton: Creative Publishing Inc., 1997.

Creasy, Rosalind. *The Edible Flower Garden*. Boston: PeriPlus Editions (HK) Ltd., 1999.

The Culinary Institute of America. *Cooking Essentials for the New Professional Chef*. New York: Van Nostrand Reinhold, 1997.

_____. *The Professional Chef's Techniques of Healthy Cooking*. New York: Van Nostrand Reinhold, 1993.

Day, A. and L. Stuckey. *The Spice Book*. New York: David White Company, 1964.

Elliot, Rose. *The Complete Vegetarian Cuisine*. New York: Parthenon Books, 1988.

Gisslen, Wayne. *Professional Cooking*. New York: John Wiley & Sons, 1983.

Givens, Meta. *Modern Encyclopedia of Cooking*. Chicago: J.G. Ferguson & Associates, 1957.

Israel, A. *Taking Tea*. Penguin Books Canada, 1987.

Idone, Christopher. *Salad Days*. New York: Random House, 1989.

Jones, J. and E. *The Book of Bread*. New York: Harper & Row Publishers, 1982.

Kapoor, S. *Professional Healthy Cooking*. New York: John Wiley & Son Inc., 1995.

Khalsa, B. *Great Vegetables from the Great Chefs*. Vancouver: Raincoast Books, 1990.

Kittler, P.G. and K. Sucher. *Food and Culture in America*. New York: Van Nostrand Reinhold, 1989.

Labensky, S., G.G. Ingram, and S.R. Labensky. *Webster's New World Dictionary of Culinary Arts*. New Jersey: Prentice Hall, 1997.

Montagne, Prosper. *Larousse Gastronomique: The Encyclopedia of Food, Wine and Cooking*. London: Hamlyn, 1961.

Reader's Digest. *Magic and Medicine of Plants*. New York: Reader's Digest Association Inc., 1986.

Stobart, T. *Herbs, Spices, and Flavorings*. New York: The Overlook Press, 1982.

Swahn, J.O. *The Lore of Spices*. London: Grange Books, 1992.

Cultivation References

Alberta Agriculture, Food, and Rural Development. *1998 Annual Report.* Edmonton: Crop Diversification Centre North, 1998.

Barash, Cathy Wilkinson. *Edible Flowers: From Garden to Palate.* Golden, Colorado: Fulcrum Publishing, 1993.

Bown, Deni. *Encyclopedia of Herbs and Their Uses.* London: Dorling Kindersley Ltd., 1995.

_____. *Growing Herbs.* London: Dorling Kindersley Ltd., 1995.

Bush-Brown, Louise and James. *America's Garden Book.* New York: MacMillan, 1996.

Crockett, James Underwood and Ogden Tanner. *Herbs.* Alexandria, Virginia: Time-Life Books, 1977.

DeBaggio, Thomas and Susan Belsinger. *Basil: An Herb Lover's Guide.* Loveland, Colorado: Interweave Press, 1996.

_____. *Growing Herbs from Seed, Cutting, and Root.* Loveland, Colorado: Interweave Press, 1994.

Gibbons, Euell. *Stalking the Healthful Herbs.* New York: David McKay Company Inc., 1966.

Hole, Lois with Jill Fallis. *Lois Hole's Bedding Plant Favorites.* Edmonton: Lone Pine Publishing, 1994.

_____. *Lois Hole's Favorite Trees & Shrubs.* Edmonton: Lone Pine Publishing, 1997.

_____. *Lois Hole's Perennial Favorites.* Edmonton, Alberta, Lone Pine Publishing, 1995.

_____. *Lois Hole's Rose Favorites.* Edmonton, Alberta, Lone Pine Publishing, 1997.

_____. *Lois Hole's Vegetable Favorites.* Edmonton, Alberta, Lone Pine Publishing, 1993.

Jacobs, Betty E.M. *Growing and Using Herbs Successfully.* Charlotte, Vermont: Garden Way Publishing, 1981.

Lancaster, Roy. *What Perennial Where.* Vancouver: Cavendish Books, 1997.

McVicar, Jekka. *Good Enough to Eat.* London: Kyle Cathie Ltd., 1997.

_____. *Jekka's Complete Herb Book.* Vancouver: Raincoast Books, 1997.

Oster, Maggie. *Ortho's All About Herbs.* Des Moines, Iowa: Meredith Books, 1999.

Shaudys, Phyllis. *Herbal Treasures.* Pownal, Vermont: Storey Communications Inc., 1990.

_____. *The Pleasure of Herbs.* Pownal, Vermont: Storey Communications Inc., 1986.

Small, Ernest. *Culinary Herbs.* Ottawa: National Research Council Press, 1997.

Smith & Hawken. *The Book of Outdoor Gardening.* New York: Workman Publishing Company, 1996.

Stuart, Malcom, ed. *The Encyclopedia of Herbs & Herbalism.* Rexdale, Ontario: Bedford Press, 1979.

Tenenbaum, Frances, ed. *Taylor's 50 Best Herbs & Edible Flowers.* New York: Houghton Mifflin Company, 1999.

Willard, Terry. *Edible and Medicinal Plants of the Rocky Mountains and Neighbouring Territories.* Calgary: Wild Rose College of Natural Healing Ltd., 1992.

Index of Recipes

Index of Species